Enhancing Presentational Effectiveness

TREY GUINN

All artwork created with love by
SHANNON GUINN

DEDICATION

This book and so much else would be impossible
without the love and support of Shannon Rose,
my wife and hiking buddy for life.

We live in constant hope that God grow our hearts
to be more like His and that we be used for His glory.

We dedicate this book to our children
and learners everywhere.

GRATITUDE

I am especially grateful for the many educators
and opportunity-creators who have invited me
into the arenas of life and onto stages big and small.

To the many individuals who have poured into my life,
I pray that you see a return on your investment and
that the person I am becoming makes you proud.

CONTENTS

PART 1

INTRODUCTION,
PROBLEM STATEMENT,
AND PREVIEW OF THE SOLUTION

CHAPTER 1

THANK YOU!
I AM SO GRATEFUL
FOR THE OPPORTUNITY
TO WRITE THIS BOOK

I hope this book finds you well. I am writing to you from a delightful hotel suite in Savannah, Georgia. I have just returned to my room after delivering a presentation to a banquet hall full of college and university administrators about *How to maximize your executive presence.* My tie is loose, and I am shamelessly enjoying an afternoon coffee with some treats that were delivered to my room. I am coming down from the standard adrenaline rush most people get after speaking before a crowd. This audience was friendly. They laughed when I hoped they would, nodded their heads on cue, and applauded loudly at the end.

Should I be embarrassed to admit I am in a good mood because of it?

The only negative about this talk is my voice is sore, which is because—true to many conference hotels—the audio in the banquet room acted wonky from the start. So, rather than play roulette with the microphone for 90 minutes, I decided in the first minute to call an audible; I put down the microphone and projected my own voice. It was the right decision, but it means my voice will sound a little bit like Al Pacino for the first hour or so after the talk.

I can't think of a better time to start writing this book than now. This book is about *enhancing presentational effectiveness*, and it ought to be written by someone who ac*tually* develops and delivers presentations regularly. This may seem obvious to you and me, but let me explain why I make this point.

At about the time I was finishing my Ph.D. and applying for professorships, I learned a few things regarding my discipline that surprised me. Like me, most of my peers and contemporaries were applying for professorships in communication programs. Such jobs often involve teaching public speaking. That part is not surprising.

What surprised me though, was learning that nearly all my peers and contemporaries despised teaching courses in public speaking and similar classes that included giving presentations. Perhaps a bit naïve of me, but I presumed people trained in human communication and public speaking would have gotten into this arena and stayed in this arena in part, if not mostly, because of the opportunity to learn and teach others the art and science of communication effectiveness.

After all, several of us were funded by generous teaching assistantships and research assistantships where we learned, thought, taught, and talked about human communication. In other words, many communication graduate students receive stipends and tuition waivers for teaching courses in public speaking. I thought we were all doing that because we liked it and thought it was fun.

Hence, I figured the job market coming out of graduate school would be cutthroat. And it was, but not because everyone was fighting to teach more public speaking courses! Instead, it turns out most people I knew couldn't wait to pass the torch the moment they got out of graduate studies or landed a professorship. This meant that I was in luck as a job candidate – most institutions I wanted to be at were seeking someone that was willing and ready to teach courses that involved human communication and public speaking.

Coming out of my doctorate, I accepted many job interviews for professorships. Several of them went quite well, resulting in more interviews and campus visits to some beautiful universities across America. One rule of mine throughout the application process was to be brutally honest about myself both on paper and in-person. A professorship has the potential to last a lifetime, and so the last thing you want to present is a phony version of yourself and feel bound to a fake you. One of the things I was very direct about on my resume and during the interviews was the amount of public speaking I do and the amount of time I invest as a communication coach and consultant.

On multiple campus visits, the individual interviewing me would be a little shocked by the amount of work I do, suggesting that it's quite a surprise I managed to do this while doing this, that, and the other. Then, they would make one of two comments. The subtle one went something like, "Well, I doubt you will find much time for that as a professor here. The demands will be too much, and the pressure for tenure yada, yada, yada." The less subtle version went something like, "As a professor here, you would not be allowed to keep that up. Doing public speaking and giving presentations to businesses is not going to fly around here yada, yada, yada."

I respect their position, but *respectfully* disagree. My response to many of them, I still believe. If I were to be a track coach, you'd probably be interested in knowing whether I am an active athlete who practices the skills I coach. If I were to teach surgery at your medical school, you'd probably want to know that I am an active surgeon and can manage the scalpel with ease.

Examples like these are endless, which emboldens my belief that someone teaching public speaking and presentational effectiveness ought to be an active public speaker—someone that presents effectively. So, while I write this book as both a student and teacher of presentational effectiveness, the majority of what I share here are insights I have learned from the stage and skills I have cultivated in the arena.

So, cheers from Savannah! Happy reading!

CHAPTER 2

THE PROBLEM:
THE MESSAGE SENT IS NOT
ALWAYS THE MESSAGE RECEIVED

It was the fall of 2000 and I was a freshman in college. I was a bit nervous as I walked across campus, making my way to my very first college course. I got to class early and was determined to take a seat in the front row. I knew I wasn't typically an A student, so sitting in the front row was my best chance of starting fresh and making a positive first impression on the professor on day one.

You may know an unspoken expectation is that the first day of a college class is usually just "syllabus day." This is when the professor engages with the students a bit, shares a few expectations for the course, and passes out the syllabus, all before ending class early and sending people on their merry way.

For some, it's a brief encounter simply meant to set the stage for what is to come. This, however, was not the case for this particular class. The professor decided to begin lecturing with course materials on day one.

After about 30 minutes passed, I looked around and saw that most of my peers were either falling asleep or, at a minimum, getting distracted.

Determined to start the semester strong and make a good impression, I fought the urge to get distracted and paid very close attention. And it's a good thing too, because the professor said something that has stuck with me ever since.

In mid-sentence, the professor stomped his foot to the ground, threw up his arm and declared "Nay, nay, nay. The message sent is not always the message received."

I looked around the room to see if anyone else was awakened to this monumental declaration. To my surprise, everyone was perfectly still as if nothing had happened. How could this be? The good professor had just said a mouthful. With one simple sentence, I was—and remain—captivated.

The message sent is not always the message received! I am sure that I already knew this. But throughout the day I kept repeating the sentence to myself and thinking about seemingly complicated situations that I could explain away by applying this uncomplicated statement. My mind was really racing.

Sure, anyone could tell you about a simple misunderstanding or misinterpretation, but my mind was entranced with questions like,

What exactly happens when the message sent is not the message received?

Just how far does this problem manifest itself?

How much damage is done at the hands of (mis)communication?

These thoughts stayed with me all semester. I recounted situations that I had lived and observed a bit differently. I can remember even asking my fellow classmates and dorm-mates if they could think of examples when the message sent was not the one received. One guy down the hall told us over dinner about how much trouble he got in over missing curfew, even though he swore it was an honest misunderstanding.

Indeed, sometimes message failures are funny to think back on when you get older, but may not be funny in the moment!

The idea that *the message sent is not always the message received* is all around us. Fans of the show <u>Friends</u> can tell you that Ross and Rachel clearly did not see eye to eye on what it meant for their relationship to be "on a break." The problem of messages sent not always equaling messages received permeated throughout the entire show, and it even constitutes much of the humor and drama surrounding many of your favorite shows.

From Main Street to Wall Street. From your house to the White House. The problem of the message sent not always being the message received is everywhere. People who keep up with current events over the years will recall infamous messages poorly received like the "Mission Accomplished" banner from President George W. Bush and the retort, "I'd like my life back" by BP CEO Tony Hayward following the deaths and devastation from the Deepwater Horizon oil spill of 2010. In these numerous accounts, I want to believe that if people knew how the message would be received, they would rethink the message being sent.

In the era of #MeToo, the most recent winter holiday was seasoned with debates from well-known figures over the messages and meanings from a holiday classic, "Baby, It's Cold Outside." Opposing sides proclaimed to hear two very different songs. Some hear the song and think of it as playful flirting between two potential lovers. Others hear the song and determine that the male character is a villain, creeping on a vulnerable female.

My point here is not to weigh in on the debate, but to highlight the existence of one. The *same song* heard by different people *means different things*. Indeed, the message sent is not always the message received.

I could go on and on with examples, or you could just turn on cable news and give it a minute or two before hearing some for yourself. The point being made is: this dilemma—the message sent is not always the message received—is pervasive. It's also quite consequential.

But how big of a concern should this be for us? Well, for a moment, take account of yourself as a communicator.

When are you communicating? Jot down below the times in a week you are communicating, delivering messages, presenting yourself and/or your ideas.

-
-
-
-
-
-
-
-
-
-

I am guessing that after a few moments you realized you are constantly communicating. From the moment you wake, you are communicating. It's not just the words you speak, it is the messages you type. Beyond that, it is the way you present yourself via your outfit and accessories to how you move and gesture.

Pause right now. Assess your attire, your posture, the look on your face. Without even murmuring a word, what information would someone gather about you if they had one glance at you right now? What opinions would they form of you? In what ways would those opinions be shaped by what you are doing? In what ways might those opinions alter based on who the observer is and what biases they carry?

That is just one freeze frame in time. If we believe such a freeze frame has the ability to convey so much information, now times that by every moment in your day, then add the actual words you speak and how you speak them...not to mention all the messages you type and send.

Suffice it to say, you are always sending and receiving messages, some intended and others not. We can't help it. We are communicative beings. While we may not always be on a stage delivering a formal address to a large audience, we are frequently, if not always, presenting ourselves—as well as making sense of others' messages and behaviors.

*"The importance of accuracy in communication is underscored by the fact that **we send and receive nonverbal messages virtually all our waking hours when we are with other people.** Though we may say nothing with words, our facial expressions, gestures, posture, body position and manner of dress continually send very telling messages. When we speak, our tone, velocity and volume of speech convey additional meaning."*
-- *New York Times (Jane E. Brody, 1992)*

If we are constantly communicating, then we are regularly sending messages that may not actually be received as we intended; and, we may regularly receive messages not as they were intended.

Now, some may be quick to say, *"Ok, I get it. We communicate all the time. But truth is I am a great communicator. I know plenty of people who should work on their communication skills and could use this book. But I am good. No problems here."*

I liken this argument to the notion of, "I understand how to eat—after all, I have been eating my whole life—and, therefore, don't need any help with eating!" It's true that we have been eating since birth and some of us may even hold the fork properly, but that does not mean we always eat the right foods at the right times and care for our bodies nutritiously.

The truth is that presentational effectiveness matters. And the problem is that most people are not as effective as they think they are or wish that they could be!

Plenty of us try to weasel around that reality. We say things like, "Well, I don't necessarily like public speaking, but it's different when I am [teaching my class; leading my meeting; speaking in front of my congregation]."

The barometer of your presentational effectiveness is not the amount of head nods you receive from a room of people that adore you, perhaps even report to you. Your captive audience knows to give you their attention, laugh at your jokes, behave as you wish they would. It's part of the human exchange. They smile and nod when you talk, and you reward them with a type of gold star.

A better test would be how well you can capture and compel an audience of people who don't owe you anything, perhaps even an audience of people who walk into your talk opposing you and/or your message.

None of us have perfected our presentational effectiveness. Each of us has room to grow. We are wise to be lifelong learners of human communication, allowing each day to teach us a bit more about our own strengths and growth areas.

My physically fit friends are the perfect example of this; no matter how "fit" they get, they always crave more knowledge about how to best improve their nutrition and strength. I try to live the same way with human communication and presentational effectiveness—because just when I think I have learned what I need to know, I come across a situation that takes me back to the drawing board.

Not long ago, I had a situation that brought to light new considerations of the problem. I was in the middle of a workday and received a text from a very close family member—so close that we regularly read each other's thoughts and finish each other's sentences.

This very close family member texted me something like: *Hey, today is John's birthday. We should take him out to eat.*

I was in a hurry to a meeting and managed to write back: *Woohoo! Sounds like fun.*

Her rapid reply was:
If you don't want to go, just say so.

Sitting in my meeting and confused, I managed to reply:
For real. You pick the restaurant. My treat.

I saw the bubbles that she was typing. The bubbles came. They left. They came back, and then her final reply:
uggghhh.

I was shocked. How did this simple text exchange go so poorly? I sat in my meeting and just kept thinking back to the principle that has haunted me since my freshman year of college. *The message sent is not always the message received.* And what was particularly disturbing was that this simple exchange was between someone that knows me incredibly well. She was supposed to get me, know my thoughts, understand the intent behind my messages.

Have you ever felt like this too? That feeling of how can you know me so well yet misunderstand me so much?!

Now, let's complicate this a bit more. Imagine that, instead of coming from a close family member, the text had come from a colleague asking me if I was available to take some other colleague out for a birthday dinner. I quickly reply in the affirmative as I had before. If they too had misunderstood my enthusiasm as sarcasm, they may have thought I was a jerk but replied neutrally with something like, "Ok, well, let me know." And I would never have known that the message sent was not received. They would have secretly rolled their eyes at me and I would have kept on going like all was well.

If life went on like this, I might easily take the sum of my interactions with others and falsely assume that (a) my family members and close loved ones misunderstand me, take my enthusiasm as sarcasm, and assume I mean things I don't actually mean, but (b) my acquaintances and colleagues actually understand me and what I am saying.

I might assume that members of my family are too sensitive, but my colleagues are easier to interact with, because they get me and never have something negative to say about me. This, of course, would be faulty reasoning.

In actuality, all people are capable of misunderstanding me. All things being equal, the messages I send are just as likely to be misconstrued by the person to my left as the person to my right. But some people, such as family members, are more likely to call me out, push back, and argue with me if the messages I am sending impact them in a way they don't like, regardless of the intentions behind the message.

Take another example to help illustrate the point. I was at the pool with my family last summer. We were splashing around and having fun. A friend snapped a cute picture of all of us, which never happens! So, I proudly posted it up on social media right then and there.

While swimming, my account started blowing up with "likes" and flattering comments. It felt affirming to see that people loved the pic of my cute family. An hour later, while still at the pool, one of my best friends calls and says, "Dang dude, were you just itching to show off those biceps? Nice!"

He was being funny, and it made me laugh. He teased me a good bit and then we caught up for a quick minute.

After we hung up, I thought about his comment a little longer. My *intent* for posting the photo was instigated by being overjoyed at having a flattering picture with my family at the pool and then wanting to share it on social media. I wanted all my happy vibes to be multiplied as people liked and praised my photo.

To be honest, it feels good when people like my family and tell me how cute we are together. That's pretty normal, right? I think most people could understand that.

But my friend's comment revealed what probably many people assumed about my intentions but would never say: "Ok Trey, we get it. You work out and want the world to know." Once that sunk in, that the message intended might not be the one received, I was mortified.

Within a few minutes from the call from my friend, I strongly considered deleting the photo, and here is why: I believe effective communicators take responsibility not just for the intentions behind their messages, but (within reason) also the impact of their message.

If the impact of posting the photo would reasonably cause people to assume that the intentions were negative, selfish, or attention-seeking, then I'd rather take down the photo than have anyone—me or you—think about it for another second.

Ultimately, I decided to leave the photo up as a social experiment and because I knew it would make a great story to tell my class. And I was right. It's become an excellent, self-deprecating example of intent versus impact and how the message sent is not always the message received.

Turns out that a couple more of my guy friends teased me in the comments section, and you can too @instaguinn. Look for the 2019 Labor Day pool pic!

...

Whether it be a text message between a family member that went awry, the social media post that my friends tease me about, or any number of experiences, I allow these instances to sharpen me as a communicator. I behave the same as a public speaker and presenter. If an audience doesn't laugh at something that I thought was funny, there must be a reason why, and rather than chalk it up as an audience problem, I need to consider ways to modify my messages and deliver them better in order to enhance my presentational effectiveness.

If you want to grow in your effectiveness as a communicator, you can't get bent out of shape when people misinterpret or dislike the messages you are sending. You have to rise above it, be willing to learn and grow, and ultimately do what is necessary (as appropriate) to accomplish your goals.

In other words, I can't just be interested in the intentions behind my messages. I have to remain invested in the impact my messages have on the recipient(s). If the message I'm sending is not the one received, that concerns me because it will affect my audience and, ultimately, me and my goals as a communicator. If a cute picture of my family causes the viewer to reasonably perceive me as being attention-seeking and showing off my physique, that is no good. Delete it.

Similarly, if the way I convey enthusiasm about taking someone to dinner causes the receiver of my text to reasonably perceive me as being sarcastic, that is no good. Reconsider the message next time. To be an effective communicator and presenter, I must be thinking about whether the message sent will be the one received.

I must be more interested in the message received than the message sent, which means I must remain more focused on my audience than myself.

To boil it down, a critical issue facing communicators is the reality that the message sent is not always the message received, and life experience tells us that we will not always know how people are receiving our messages. But in order to be effective communicators, we must be invested in the message others receive from us, not just the messages we believe we are sending.

The first step in fixing a problem is acknowledging the possibility of one. So, can you reason with me that it is possible you may not be as great a communicator as you think you are and that you, like me and everyone around us, has the capacity to enhance our presentational effectiveness.

If you are open to the ideas shared thus far, this book is for you. Keep reading!

CHAPTER 3

A PROBLEM THIS BIG
NEEDS A SIMPLE SOLUTION:
DEMONSTRATE WILLINGNESS

"According to most studies, people's number one fear is public speaking. Number two is death. Death is number two... This means to the average person, if you go to a funeral, you are better off in the casket than doing the eulogy." - Jerry Seinfeld

When speaking to crowds on presentational effectiveness, I usually ask for a quick show of hands to see how many people in the room dislike or altogether avoid public speaking. Rarely will any hands go up. I will then ask the same crowd for a show of hands to see how many people like or seek opportunities to give presentations. A handful of people will raise their hands.

Even with a highly extroverted group, only about 25% of the people express desire to do public speaking. Do the math on that, and you will quickly realize the irony. A ton of hands should have gone up on the first question, yet people who avoid public speaking tend to be the same ones who avoid raising their hands, in fear that doing so will draw attention to them—or worse, the speaker might call on them and urge them to participate, which is the very thing they were avoiding in the first place!

One way or another, I always manage to get at least one volunteer to join me on the stage and read aloud the Seinfeld quote from the opening of this chapter. Right as they near the end, on perfect cue, the speaker and audience will almost always share a good laugh. It's like clockwork. As the last words are being read, the laughter from the room sets in. Nearly every time. While the entire room gets a great laugh, the fringe benefit is that the otherwise nervous presenter gets to experience the infectious joy of making a room laugh.

The quote itself is funny because it points out a truth—most people avoid public speaking at all costs. Fewer people than you may realize are willing to be the one to take the stage and deliver the message.

The first step to enhancing presentational effectiveness is: BE WILLING.

You read that right, and it really is as simple as it sounds. But years of experience have taught me that it bears mentioning. If you are not first willing to enhance your presentational effectiveness, then there is no need to talk about the steps for improving your abilities.

I was an early adopter of the first-generation iPad, and I've owned one ever since. Most days, my iPad is near my MacBook and not far from my Apple Watch and iPhone. I get giddy over seeing all my devices sync, yet I wonder how long it'll be until I stop using a computer altogether and go all-in on the iPad.

That said, I've purchased quite a few iPads over the years for family, friends, and coworkers because I believe they are such powerful tools that I want others to benefit from too! Sometimes this works out as planned, and I see someone will make the most of the gift given. I've known others to thank me, play with it a bit, and then leave it on a shelf for collecting dust and cobwebs.

The truth of the matter is that some people prefer to not use an iPad, and I should probably figure that out before going and buying them one!

I can send them tips and tricks and how-to videos all day on how to unlock the potential of such a powerful machine, but towards what aim? My best efforts and intentions are wasted until the person that now owns the device decides they are *willing* to embrace and maximize the device.

As someone who teaches other people about how to enhance their presentational effectiveness, I have learned that before teaching them how to, I should probably figure out if they want to and are willing to first. Some people want to enhance their presentational effectiveness but are convinced they cannot and therefore will not try.

I know a little about what this feels like. As a young person, I loved cars—especially the Porsche 911. I would read about them and cut out pictures of them from magazines. When old enough to drive, I would regularly stop by fancy car lots to just walk near and occasionally sit in one.

One day, my friend's dad asked me if I wanted to drive his Porsche. I froze for a minute, then politely declined. Of course, anyone who knows me could tell you that I definitely *wanted* to drive the car, but when I was confronted with the opportunity, it turned out that I was nervous as heck.

The car of my dreams seemed beyond my reach, and now the keys were being handed over. But I didn't have the self-confidence to grab them and go. So, instead of seizing the moment, I asked if he would be willing to take me for a spin. I missed out big time.

I would have loved every minute of driving the car; and knowing myself, I would have returned it safely, filled the tank with gas, and even wiped it spotless when I was done. But I missed the opportunity out of insecurity and fear.

I've had clients and audience members do similar things when faced with an opportunity to present. They want to enhance their presentational effectiveness, and then when given a chance to take the stage and speak on behalf of their team, they pass the ball to someone else and say something like, "Oh, *me* give the presentation? No, it's ok. Jane is the better speaker, so she should probably do it."

This is about the equivalent of me turning to my friend's dad and saying, "Oh, *me* drive your Porsche? No it's ok. Uhhh... since you know the car so much better than me... would you be willing to take me for a spin instead?"

There may be many reasons why a person would be unwilling to try public speaking and put themselves in a position to enhance their presentational effectiveness. One explanation worthy of our consideration has to do with mindset.

Most of what we understand regarding *mindset* is often credited to Carol Dweck, renowned Stanford Psychologist. Here goes my attempt at summing up decades of research in a couple sentences: whereas individuals with a fixed mindset believe their basic abilities and talents are fixed traits that are incapable of being developed, those with a growth mindset understand that their talents and abilities can be developed through effort, good teaching, and persistence.

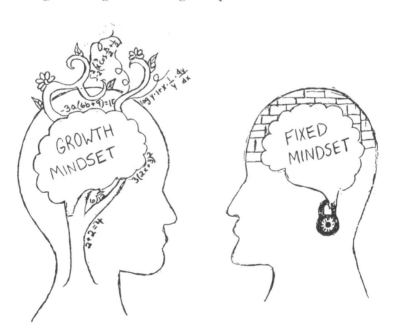

This is not to say all people can become geniuses, but fundamentally, everyone can get smarter and better if they work at it.

I imagine most of us are prone to believing we operate from a growth mindset, and we probably think life must be a little sadder for those who operate with a fixed mindset. Personally, I would love to think you, me, and everyone everywhere demonstrated a growth mindset. I would love if we all rejected even the slightest tendencies of a fixed mindset. However, my own experiences and observations have shown me that the traps of a fixed mindset are more pervasive than we might initially imagine.

For instance, consider the concept of a *math person*. Ever heard someone say a phrase like, "I'm not much of a math person", or said another way, "he's a real math person." This very notion that some of us are math people while others of us are not is evidence of a fixed mindset.

As a young person, I was utterly convinced that I was not a math person. Most of my teachers perpetuated this very myth. By sixth grade, I learned what to do when I saw a hard math problem. I would either guess the answer, turn to a "math person" for help (aka the answer), or scratch my head and look confused just long enough for a teacher to come and help.

Later in life, I learned the truth of what makes a math person—they are the ones who do the math problems. When they get stuck, they consult the book, ask for clarification, and give the question a little more time. Ultimately, they work through it and figure out math problems one at a time, thus gaining the knowledge and skills to tackle the next set of problems. This being said, their growth mindset is reason for them to stick with it and do the math, thereby becoming a math person. Dweck's research explains this in spectacular detail.

Math wasn't the only area of my life where I lied to myself. "I'm just not a runner" and "I'm not built for running" are phrases I repeated to myself and said aloud on numerous occasions for most of my life.

If I were asked to join a friend on a run, I would politely decline by insisting that I would only slow them down. I would frequently reference how I'd get side stitch when I started running or I would give a nod to my allergies and how breathing was really difficult for me when running because of my allergies, etc.

My mindset was that I had tried running a few times throughout my life and could endure it momentarily, but ultimately, I was not a runner like others I knew. Hence, I hardly ever ran, and definitely not by choice or for fun.

Eventually, someone set me straight. It was a friendly call out by a loved one. She said to me, "Trey, the reason you're not a runner is because you don't run." She elaborated about how everyone's breathing is rough when they start out, and slight discomforts like side stitch are normal for new runners, but all stuff goes away once you work through it. If true, this meant that setting aside dire circumstances and legitimate limitations, if someone wants to be a runner, all they must do is lace their shoes and run. I was not fully convinced, but I was willing to try.

So, for about a month, I woke up earlier than usual, laced my shoes, and jogged around my neighborhood.

It was dark and no one could see me; I ran up and down the streets the best I could. The first week was rough, but I had a hunch the second week would be better. So, I pressed on. By week three, I could jog through the discomfort, and improvements were obvious to me. By the end of the first month, I would wake up eager to lace my shoes. And I have been running ever since.

That is a big deal for a guy who spent 30 years of his life convincing himself and others that he was not a runner. It has confirmed for me, quite personally, the power of mindset. The individual who believes they are not a math person is not going to even try and solve the math problem. The person who claims "I am not a runner" will not even lace their shoes and press through the first week of discomfort.

Similarly, as a public speaking instructor and communication coach, I have noticed that there are many who say something like, "Um, someone else can do it; not me. I am not much of a presenter." Guess what I tell them?

*"You aren't a presenter
...because you don't present."*

Therefore, before evaluating our abilities as a speaker, we must first check our mindset. Do you think of delivering presentations from a fixed or growth mindset? Do you avoid public speaking because, ultimately, you believe you aren't a public speaker? If so, you're right; you aren't a public speaker, and you won't become one until you do some public speaking.

Next time there's a call for volunteers, throw up your hand and go for it. The evidence suggests that the benefits are plenty. I frequently tell audiences—what we have known to be true for decades now, thanks to research conducted by scholars like Jim McCroskey, John Daly, and many who have followed— that a person's mere willingness to communicate is consequential of how others see them. The simplest explanation is this: individuals that show greater willingness to communicate—lead the group meeting, deliver the presentation, offer a mealtime toast or prayer—are more likely to be considered the influential person in the room, the socially and sexually attractive person amongst their peers. Notice here that your *mere willingness to communicate* is enough to positively shape others' opinions of you (of course, the more capable and talented the better, but we will get to that soon).

Findings like these remind me of my freshman year of college. Our residence hall was a popular place for freshman to eat and congregate throughout the day. It helped that our hall had the best food on campus! And on days when the weather outside was particularly pleasant, one of my roommates was notorious for finishing dinner early, grabbing his guitar from our room, and making his way outside.

He would proceed to find a comfortable step at the entrance of the building, ditch his shirt, and strum his guitar.

And guess what? No matter what he played or how well he played it, the response was positive. He started making new friends as a result. Girls began to talk about the cute guitar guy. I repeat, it did not matter what he played or how well he played it, the response was always positive.

And like the research referenced earlier, if I had surveyed all within our vicinity, I am confident that the results would show that he was considered to be more socially and sexually attractive than the rest of us. Not because he was unusually handsome and charming or especially talented on the guitar. He was winning in the court of public opinion simply because he was willing.

People like my college roommate—the ones who dig deep and find the inner courage to put themselves out there—will tell you that willingness begets willingness. And even more, it's the spark that lights a fire within. When a good person with the right motives demonstrates willingness and puts themselves out there, the response is more than likely going to be positive, and those around them will literally or figuratively cheer them on.

As you observe and receive positive feedback from others, confidence and self-assurance within you grows, which is capable of breeding greater willingness. It's an amplifying loop wherein willingness begets willingness.

CHAPTER 4

AND THIS SOLUTION TOO: DEVELOP READINESS

The problem with presentational effectiveness is partly explained by the reality that messages sent are not always the messages received. We have established that communication hiccups and problems are real, pervasive, and can be consequential. One critical component to addressing this reality is we become willing communicators—the types of people who say, "Sure, I will be glad to give the presentation next week."

While demonstrating willingness is step one in solving the communication conundrum, developing readiness is what leads to next level greatness.

Think of it like the running example I gave earlier. Sure, it is true that I would never have become a runner without being someone who was willing to lace my shoes and go for a run. Eventually, I started to think more about my overall performance as a runner. This was due, in part, because some of the people that I would run with seemed to know things that I didn't know. They paced themselves, trained smarter, and ran a little faster (ok, a lot faster).

While we were both demonstrating the willingness to run, it was undeniable that they were better runners than me. They showed up to morning workouts and weekend races ready to run well—and they did.

In this way, running and presenting are similar. There can be no victory in presenting or running without a willingness to show up and try, but truth be told, there are some who perform better than others. Now, how we measure this is not always the same. Scanning some stat sheets suggests that running performance is purely quantifiable—distance, time, splits, pace, place, etc. Fastest runner wins.

Yet our sense-making of the world tells us that not all running performance looks and feels the same. No matter how much faster I get, I have yet to find one picture of me running that is remotely flattering.

Contrary, my wife and some of my running buddies have race-day pictures that should be on magazine covers. Their muscles are chiseled, and their breathing appears effortless.

Some people just make running look cool. With all things equal and speeds the same, the people running to my left and right are far more likely than me to have a flattering running photo.

So, if running is about speed, numbers do not lie. But if there is more to running than being the fastest, we ought to consider other variables. In this way, again, running and presenting are quite similar. Surely presenting is not just about who can convey the most information in the least amount of time or who can stand on a stage the longest.

In fact, while there are things about presentational effectiveness that are quantifiable, there are also elements to presentational effectiveness that have more to do with the look, the feel, the vibe, and all those things that require more than just numbers and stat sheets.

So, as we begin to explore this notion of enhancing our presentational effectiveness, I put the question to you:

What makes for an effective presentation?

Or, consider the other side of the same coin:

What makes for an ineffective presentation?

Think back to the presentations that have impressed you most, and also the ones that have impressed you least. Give the following questions a few minutes, and then list a few things:

Which individuals come to mind when you consider great presenters?

-

-

Likewise, what are some memorable presentations? What make them particularly memorable for you?

-

-

What kinds of words/phrases come to your mind when you consider effective presentations and effective presenters?

-

-

What kinds of words/phrases come to your mind when you consider ineffective presentations and ineffective presenters?

-

-

As I travel around and talk to people about questions like these, I receive some familiar feedback. When calling out what makes for an effective presentation, people will often point to "being prepared" and "knowing your stuff."

For all the years I have asked audience members these questions, I would venture to say the most frequent response has something to do with being prepared. Even more, people usually tell me that when they are prepared, they do great; conversely, when they are not prepared, they struggle.

I will occasionally ask people how they prepare, and what good preparation entails. Sadly, I am afraid many individuals begin preparing for a speech in all the wrong ways.

There are a lot of ways people "prepare" that are not helping the cause for presentational effectiveness.

Asking yourself, "What do I want to say?" is not the way to begin preparing. Googling funny photos/videos for your slides is not the right way to prepare. Looking for long YouTube clips to kill the time is not the way to prepare.

I also receive a lot of feedback about how effective presenters are "confident" and "make presentations relatable to their audience." Sometimes I get very specific feedback like, "speakers should have good eye contact" and "presenters need to project their voices." And I agree with all this feedback.

The interesting thing is much of our ability to understand presentational effectiveness does not require years and years of study. I find that most people can articulate what they believe constitutes presentational effectiveness or what they think great presenters do. I hear a few diverging thoughts, but most of the feedback is pretty similar.

The point of this book is not necessarily to impose one particular view about how to spot a great public speaker. Instead, I am really interested in helping us enhance our own presentational effectiveness by simplifying our understanding of what it is and how to most easily achieve it.

Toward that end, you will need to keep reading!

TREY GUINN

PART 2

TREY'S TRIANGLE:
A VERY PRESENT HELP
IN TIME OF NEED

I don't like to over-complicate things. For me, simple and memorable solutions are far preferable over complicated ones that are impossible to remember, much less implement.

When first hired to manage projects and lead people, I got ambitious, bought a coffee, and took a stroll through my local bookstore in hopes of finding a helpful read—something to get me jazzed up and ready for my new job! I recall walking through the management and leadership sections and finding titles that read something like, *The 35 Undeniable Laws of Leadership* and *The 25 Must-dos for Making the Most of your Management Matrix.*

I was overwhelmed. I barely remember to eat lunch most days. How am I supposed to go throughout my day keeping up with dozens of undeniable laws and rules for effective anything?

So, while I live as a consummate student of human communication and presentational effectiveness, I teach it to my students and clients in the simplest way possible.

This triangle is what I consider before each phone call I make, email I send, presentation I deliver, and so forth. It is the same triangle I have taught to CEOs, university presidents, professional athletes, and thousands of others.

There is no sparkle or shine. The beauty, instead, is in the simplicity. And the benefit, as you will soon discover, is in the usability.

And so, I present to you Trey's Triangle:

Pretty incredible, right?

Just kidding.

For real this time, I present to you:

*Every communicative act begins with a **Goal**. Attainment of your goal is dependent on **Audience Perception** of your **Message** (the content) and **You** (your delivery).*

CHAPTER 5

GOAL:
THE PURPOSE OF MY SPEECH
IS TO _____.

Every presentation should have a purpose, a goal. Without one, why are you talking? What is the point? As the communicator, you must begin with a baseline assumption: you want something from your audience/listener. If you don't have a goal, why are you communicating? Have you ever sat through a presentation, a meeting, or read an email, and half-way through thought to yourself one of the following:

"What is he even saying right now?"
"What is this email even about?"
"I don't get it. What is the point?"
"I don't understand why this is my issue"

"Why exactly did you stop by to see me?"
"Well, that was a total waste of time."
"Am I supposed to do something with all this?"

I bet you think those thoughts more than you even realize. The funny thing is we often think these thoughts or whisper them to our friend when *receiving* messages, but we seem to overlook such thoughts when *sending* messages. I hope that does not seem too harsh, but chances are that if you have had that thought about someone else, then someone else has had the thought about you.

So, read the phrases again. These are the thoughts people are prone to thinking when sitting in a meeting, listening to a speech, or checking their inbox. One of our goals should be to never give someone a reason to think those thoughts about us.

Message receivers don't think those thoughts because they are rude and judgmental. They do it because, as sense-making individuals, they are constantly trying to understand the world around them. Most people perceive that their lives are massively important. Therefore, they hate to think their time is wasted. So, within the first sentence or two, they are seeking to resolve the riddle — What is the message here, and why does it matter to me?

Even altruistic others, the kind and servant-hearted in our communities, just want to know — what do you want, and how can I be most helpful? So, if they read your long email or bit through your presentation and can't figure out what you want, then at best they reach the conclusion of your message thinking, "Well, he seemed like a nice guy, but I am not sure what he wants me to do. And come to think of it, I am not even sure what the point of the message was."

Before you start drafting your message, you must get very clear about your goal. What do you want from your audience? Wanting something from your audience and having a goal for communicating doesn't make you bad or selfish. A goal for your communication can be any number of things. I am [writing you, calling you, speaking to you] today to:

- *Raise money*
- *Win a vote*
- *Persuade a room*
- *Be liked*
- *Gain respect*
- *Show leadership*
- *Convey information*
- *Make a friend*
- *Demonstrate care*
- *Recruit volunteers*
- *Convince colleagues to meet me for lunch at my favorite café*

A goal for communicating can be any number of things. Think of your presentational self just this past week. Sometimes we wear a nice outfit with the intent of wanting to impress someone. That is a goal. Know it and own it.

Sometimes we stand before a room of people to encourage that they vote in a way that we wish they would. Know your goal and own it.

Sometimes we send a note to someone for no reason other than to maintain friendship. That too is a goal. Whatever your goal, know it, own it, and let it guide you as you prepare the content and delivery of your message. The goal should drive your content and delivery.

Sadly, in many cases, the communicator seems to stumble upon a goal while delivering the actual message. How much do we dread when someone finishes their big presentation with something like, "Well, I guess we didn't really need to meet today. Everyone just keep on keeping on."

When I am working with someone and they are about to practice their presentation with me, I always start by asking them to first tell me the goal of their presentation. They usually ask what I mean. I tell them to finish the sentence, "The purpose of my speech is to_____." If it's not a speech but instead a memo or something else, just exchange the word speech with whatever communication you are preparing.

The purpose of my communication is to _____.

Until you can fill in the blank, you've got nothing. For example, I was recently speaking in San Francisco to a healthcare company that invited me to facilitate a professional development seminar. To prepare, I had to ask myself what my goals would be. I determined it was something like: *The purpose of my presentation is to enhance audience members' understanding of executive presence, to compel my audience to incorporate the critical takeaways into their daily lives, and for my audience to remember me and my presentation favorably so they will consider inviting me back!*

When was the last time you delivered a presentation? What was your purpose? Can you state your purpose in one declarative statement? If not, that is a problem.

If the purpose of your presentation isn't clear to you, how can it possibly be clear to your audience?

The next time you are presenting on stage or communicating via email, phone, or whatever it may be, demand yourself to get very clear about your purpose and goal. And be able to complete the sentence: *The purpose of my communication is to _____.*

You can have more than one goal, but each of them should be simple and stated clearly. And most importantly, all your prep and development should be centered and focused on accomplishing your goals.

As you review your work, a great question to ask yourself is, "How does this help me accomplish my stated goal(s)?" Anything not advancing your goal is potentially betraying it. Cute but distracting anecdotes, images, and side points are wasted effort, perhaps even self-defeating, unless they serve your goal.

Returning to our running metaphor, to have a communication goal is like eyeing the finish line. When running a race, runners don't just run in any direction they choose and declare to be done when they tire out. No, there is an established finish line and path between the start and end of the race. Knowing your goal (finish line) will give you a sense of direction and guide your steps.

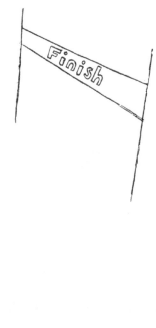

To enhance presentational effectiveness, communicators must have a clear goal in mind and develop the content and delivery of their message in a way that best supports reaching their finish line. A runner without a finish line—like a speaker without a goal—is prone to wandering off, going in circles, and venturing into oblivion. At the end, we might say, "Well, I know he was running, but I just don't have any idea where he was going." This is quite similar to the feedback I hear people say about many presentations they sit through, emails they receive, and meetings they attend.

Toward enhancing your presentation effectiveness, always have a goal. Before you do any prep work of any kind, know your goal, say it aloud, and commit it to memory.

It's simple, but worth repeating. The next time you will be presenting information of any kind via any medium, force yourself to first finish this sentence:

The purpose of my communication
is to _____.

And once you know your goal, you can begin thinking about the next critical component: your audience. For more about that, keep reading!

TREY GUINN

CHAPTER 6

AUDIENCE:
NEVER WRITE A LOVE LETTER
TO WHOM IT MAY CONCERN

"(Preparing your message) without an audience in mind is like writing a love letter and addressing it to whom it may concern." - Ken Haemer (AT&T)

Knowledge about your audience and their likely perception of you and your message should wield extraordinary influence on the development and delivery of your presentation. Many individuals fail to realize this or get lazy and will determine that presentations are like hospital gowns—one size fits most. Here is a clue: they aren't. Savvy presenters understand that knowing their audience is critical to accomplishing their goal.

> To whom it may concern,
>
> If I don't tell you this now, I think I will burst. I am so completely, deeply, desperately, madly in love with you. You have turned my whole world upside down, and I can't imagine going a single day without you. Please tell me you feel the same way.
>
> ♡ Yours truly, ♡
> Patrick

About a decade ago, I was hired by an international bank to deliver a 4-hour workshop on leadership and communication to a room full of their high-potential managers. In other words, these people had been chosen to be part of this workshop because they were high performers seen as having promise for upward mobility within the organization.

Now, it is important to note here that just the month prior I had given a similar type of talk to a similar type of crowd. *Or so I thought.* And because of this poor assumption, I walked into this presentation confident that my material would be great just the way it was—that I would not need to change much of my message content from one talk to the other.

Within 30 minutes, I realized I was completely mistaken. The first group from the month before worked traditional management roles at an investment bank, wherein they spent lots of time in face-to-face work with colleagues and clients; that group wanted and got a workshop on how to improve communication skills and practices in such a setting.

As it turned out, the second group was a collection of individuals who did most of their work from private cubicles. Much of their day consisted of datasets, emails, and making international calls while wearing a headset. And while the titles and descriptions of the workshops I was giving were nearly identical, the workshop that these two groups envisioned were quite different.

My mistake was I did not learn that until I was already 30-minutes into a four-hour workshop. I learned it the hard way. After making an important point about developing courage to present your ideas and then teaching some useful exercises for developing confidence in public speaking, an audience member threw up his hand and said, "That's really good to know, but how does that help me in my actual job? What kind of communication skills can you share with me for what I do?"

The guy asking the question saved the day. Without his question, I would not have known to course correct the workshop. And because of him, I took five minutes to ask more questions to my audience about the challenges and pain-points they face in their jobs relating to human communication. I quickly learned what I needed to know in order to change direction, salvage the talk, and win over the crowd. But I nearly lost my audience completely, and it would have been entirely my fault. Unbeknownst to me, I was mistakenly giving a great talk to the wrong audience.

The lessons I learned from this situation have been game changing. From then on, I never make the mistake of assuming to know my audience. Before agreeing to speak somewhere, I never ask just the basics—when, where, duration of talk, size of audience, and so on.

Before any of that, I ask my point of contact (who is usually the person booking me to speak) to elaborate on what they envision for the talk, what would constitute a successful talk, and how we will know that the talk was a success.

And then I ask specific questions about the audience. Who are these people? What's in it for them? I want to understand why they are coming to hear me speak. Do they even want to attend? Or are they being told to attend? What will they have been doing the night before, the day of, and just after I speak? What is the climate in their place of work? How often do they attend workshops and talks? How well do the people in the room know one another? And so forth.

I want to know their professional and personal pain-points. And I want to figure out how I can align my talk to connect to those pain-points, such that my goals as a speaker are coordinated appropriately with their hopes and expectations as an audience member.

That doesn't mean I only want to meet their expectations; in fact, sometimes I want to violate their expectations. If they are dreadfully expecting a boring four-hour seminar on communication research, then I want to positively violate that expectation by facilitating an interactive session loaded with meaningful and practical takeaways.

...

Knowing your audience is critical to accomplishing your goal. After all, they—not you— ultimately determine if you reach the goals set for your presentation!

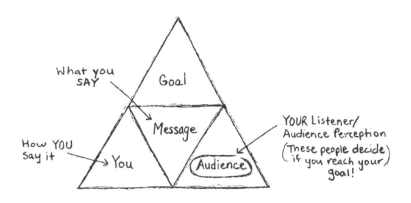

Knowledge about your audience and their likely perception of you and your message should wield extraordinary influence on the development and delivery of your presentation. In knowing your audience, you can't just know who they are and what they do. You have to understand where your talk fits within their lives. What is the socio-emotional temperature in the room? Do they love their organization? Are they in the midst of turmoil? Is this audience hostile to you and your thoughts? Or are they generally warm to you and what you will say?

One of the memorable presentations I've studied is a speech by the late Senator Ted Kennedy given on October 3, 1983 at Liberty Baptist College (now known as Liberty University) on "Faith, Truth and Tolerance in America." What is remarkable to me, and I imagine anyone who watches it, is how effectively Senator Kennedy presented himself and his ideas to *that* audience.

Kennedy, a figurehead of American liberalism, stood before an audience of proud conservatives. Yet he found a way to masterfully connect with his audience and on what could have been a politically divisive topic—faith, truth, and tolerance in America. The President and founder of the university, Jerry Falwell, remarked, "When he spoke to Liberty University students, he was well received. Even though the students did not agree with much of what he said, they were polite and kind."

More than that, it is obvious in watching the presentation from start to finish that Kennedy wooed his audience by balancing vulnerability with boldness and by celebrating shared values while also being honest about political differences. I doubt members of the audience left the arena changing their political beliefs, but you can see that the audience felt closer to the speaker and therefore were more willing to listen and consider commonality above difference.

It is a masterclass performance. I hope you will take the time to search and watch the speech. You will find that Kennedy won over his audience brilliantly. But it wasn't because of who he was or what he believed in. It was because he developed and delivered the presentation for his audience. He did not merely address his standard talking points to whom it may concern. No, he addressed *this* presentation to *that* audience.

By doing so, he clearly won over the audience and compelled them to receive him and his message with an openness that otherwise would have been denied him.

Kennedy took the time to put himself in the shoes of the audience—to understand their thoughts and feelings before assuming to impose his own onto them.

Kennedy is not the first to understand the power of knowing his audience. Marcus Cicero, the famously outspoken Roman politician, is credited for saying:

"If you wish to persuade me, you must think my thoughts, feel my feelings, and speak my words."
-Cicero (lived from 106-44 BC)

I encourage you to jot that quote down and keep it with you. It is a helpful reminder that the path to your goal is to persuade your audience, not you. You are already persuaded, but to persuade them you must know them and understand how they will perceive you and your message. Understanding your audience is how you shape message content and master your delivery.

While the fool begins working on their presentation by asking "What do I want to say?", the effective presenter asks themselves, "To accomplish my goal, what does my audience need me to deliver?"

CHAPTER 7

MESSAGE CONTENT: WHATCHA GONNA DO WITH ALL THAT JUNK?

After you have had time to define and refine your communication goals and have conducted your due diligence on your audience, it is time to begin thinking about how to develop and deliver the winning message. Now, you can begin thinking about stuff like:

"What should I say?"

"How should I say it?"

While this may invigorate you, this is usually when several of my clients start feeling overwhelmed and when the anxiety sets in. One explanation is that the work required seems daunting, but another explanation is worth considering too.

Consider that I have never been asked to give a presentation about baseball. Do you know why? It is because I know very little about baseball. I've watched some games and been to some legendary stadiums, but even then, I know very little about the sport and how to play it.

Because I know very little about the subject, I have very little I could say about it. In this way, it would be the easiest speech to give. I need zero prep time. I am ready right now: "Hey everyone! Today I want to talk to you about baseball, a sport I've never played and seldom watched. Take a look at some pictures of the stadiums I have visited and players I have met. And lastly, here is a hall of fame ball signed by a dear family friend. And well, that's all I've got for you. So, with that, thank you for your time, and I'll be happy to take your questions."

If asked to share information about the sport of baseball, that is literally all of the content I have to work with. Conversely, if someone asked me to give a presentation on running—something I do every day—I now have to stop and think about it.

A flood of ideas and memories start overwhelming my brain. Even more, if you ask me to stand up and start giving a workshop on parenting—something I live and breathe daily and care so deeply about—I would initially struggle to sort through the pile-on of thoughts and feelings.

But more often than not, this is what you are faced with when developing and delivering a message—whether that is from a stage or typing a message and clicking send. The responsibility to bear the message did not fall on you because you know little about the subject (e.g., like me with baseball), but instead it's your message to craft and share because you know and/or care so much (e.g., like me with parenting). So, with a head full of ideas, and likely a library of material to work from, we must do as the Black Eyes Peas taught us and ask ourselves, "Whatcha gonna do with all that junk?"

This is often the case for why some people struggle and procrastinate when crafting the content. You know so much about the issue that it isn't simple and easy to work with. If delivering a message is like bringing a glass of water to someone, it'd be easy for me to serve up a glass of baseball water. Because regardless of the goal and audience, I can contain what I know in just a few sentences. But to serve up a glass of parenting, I am not working from a jug of water to condense into a glass to share; I am swimming in the ocean.

Imagine some of the activities that you do the most frequently, care about the most, excel at, and are practically synonymous with your very name—like a sport or instrument you play. Now, imagine that you've got to give an 8-minute presentation to a room of people who know little to nothing about this, and you must give a clear and compelling explanation of what it is, how it works, why it is so important, and why others should do it too.

At first, most people would feel lucky that, if they must give a presentation, at least it's about something they know and love. But then as they start working on it, they will likely find that, because they are swimming in that ocean of information and experiences, it's actually difficult to effectively capture the best of what they know, and then bring it as a simple glass of water to an audience of less knowledgeable, less interested, and yet-to-be convinced others.

This is why my clients will often come to me and say, "Okay, I've got all this content that I need to cover. Now, what do I do with it?" In other words, they know the goal is X and the intel on the audience is Y, but they are working from an ocean of information, and they just don't know how to package it. And even worse, it's a topic they could speak about for hours, but they've been given only 20 minutes to present.

Some people wisely recognize the dilemma and find a solution. Others will mistakenly just force everything they know into the presentation (or email), and it will drive their audience (or reader) crazy.

I think this is something we can actually learn as children. Take for instance any given weekend at my house. Imagine a Sunday afternoon. We've just returned from brunch, and I walk back to my daughters' room. All over the floor, huge piles of clothes are tossed about and left out. Huge messes. Only a skilled gymnast could enter this room without landing on heaps of clothing. I politely urge my daughters to clean up their room and put all their clothes away.

A few minutes later, I come back to check on things. To my pleasant surprise, there are no clothes on the ground! But as I go to open their drawers, I find a hot mess of stuff. Items stuffed and shoved so much that no single item can be distinguished from another.

In other words, they took everything they had and made it fit into the drawer.

A lot of times when I hear presentations or read an email, I wonder if the author or speaker is doing to their message what my daughters do with their clothes. Take whatever you've got and cram it into somewhere else.

You want me to send out an update on the status of a project? Sure, let me just type everything that comes to my mind in one long stream-of-conscious and then click send.

You want me to do a re-cap presentation on this new material we are learning about? Sure, let me just stand on the stage and regurgitate something we already read.

You get the point, I am sure. Anyone can take piles of information and move them from one spot to another. It takes no great effort or skill to do that. It's like watching my kids move a pile of clothes from the floor to the drawer. We can check a box, but what good has it really accomplished?

I bet without thinking too hard about it, you can picture an email you've received or presentation you've sat through where the speaker had a bunch of content and did something with it. They shoved it into a long e-mail or presentation. And when it's over, you are left thinking, "Ok, to make any sense of this, I need a cup of coffee and an hour to sort through this pile of information." *(Great, clothes are in the drawer, but now we need to sort and fold them to make any sense of what's what.)*

In reality, the messenger has done us no favors. They've merely checked the box—they delivered a presentation (or sent an email) to you that contained a big messy pile of information. No one wins.

My hope is that you never commit such a crime. Be better than kids "cleaning" their room and more effective than people who simply data dump and word vomit information via email and presentations.

Although you may be working with an ocean of information or piles of mess, you may be surprised to find you can fit everything you need into the drawer quite effectively if you are willing to do the work and sort it out.

*The remainder of this chapter focuses on the importance of developing an audience-centered message that is **clear, concise, and compelling**.*

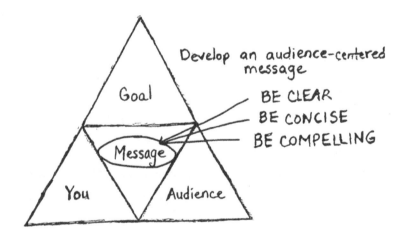

Be clear

Clarity matters. And it doesn't just matter if it's clear for you. Again, it matters that it's clear for your audience. I love the phrase and quote I've heard before from the former CEO of Procter & Gamble:

"Give it to me in the Sesame Street version."

I like the quote so much because it is counterintuitive to one of the abiding fears most public speakers face. Many of my clients and students fear sounding simple and are desperate to appear smart. I actually think a better way to describe it is that most presenters struggle with the fear of sounding dumb.

Somewhere in many of our minds is this voice saying, "Your audience thinks that you are dumb. They are rolling their eyes and laughing at you." The presenter, the one developing and delivering the message, is left worrying, "Will they all find out I am a fraud, an imposter, and that I don't belong on this stage?"

With a head full of worry and fear, the insecure presenter will play it safe, recite big and bolded information that someone else deemed important, regurgitate a bunch of already known information, and perhaps even stand behind a podium and read from text-heavy slides. In such case, the only clarity offered by the presenter is they have revealed all the clear signs for a boring presentation.

There are some obvious reasons why people wrestle with keeping a message simple and delivering it in the "Sesame Street" version. One might be, "I actually don't understand the material well enough to simplify it for my audience." Well, if that's the case, get back in the books, and get back to understanding.

If, however, the speaker is thinking, "I want to make sure I sound smart," or, "I'm afraid I'll end up sounding dumb if I don't use all the big words," then I highly urge that person to rethink their strategy.

We must bust the ridiculous myth that simplifying the message makes a person sound stupid.

What the former CEO of Procter & Gamble understood so well was that the person who can present it to me in the "Sesame Street version" has wrestled with the material so well that they have broken it down, simplified it, and can now effectively serve it to me in the clearest and most digestible form.

Quite the contrary. In all the cases I can think of, to speak simple and with clarity is to show you understand deeply, and it delights the receiver of your message. I find that only the true subject matter experts can simplify material into digestible components for their audience.

Following the presentation, a savvy presenter can answer challenging and complicated questions about their material, but that doesn't mean they present their information in a complicated way that is challenging to understand. The developed presentation ought to be simple and easy to follow like a story. This is because:

Being audience-centered means presenting your big idea clearly and quickly; not making people work hard to understand you.

In the aim toward simplifying the message, sometimes you need additional tools to help ensure that your audience connects with your idea. When you and your audience aren't on the same page, a well-timed metaphor is the homerun ball that can bridge the knowledge gap and save the day (*excessive metaphor use intended*)!

Master the metaphor

A few years ago, I was on a hike with my daughters. It was a beautiful destination, a calm day, and nothing but good vibes all around us. I didn't know the area well, but my friend who invited us was a trail pro. About a half-mile into the hike, my friend looks back to tell us something like, "Hey, keep your eyes peeled. People are saying they've seen snakes around this part of the trail."

This was about the worst thing I could have imagined hearing my friend say, as I have what some may call a phobia of snakes. The situation got worse when my four-year-old daughter looked up at me and said, "Daddy, what's a snake?"

I was kind of confused. I didn't understand why, at four years old, she didn't know what a snake was. Then again, I am afraid of them; so, it's not like we keep them in the house.

Anyway, as I was shaking the panic from my face and searching for the right words to say, my older daughter looks over very nonchalant and says, "Don't worry about it. But they're really scary. And if they bite you, you die."

In an instant, my youngest daughter leapt into my arms and buried her face into my shoulder. This was not a very fun moment during our vacation, and without an immediate redirect of conversation, I could foresee this whole adventure turning into a disaster really fast.

I knew I had to reclaim the conversation, but just like pacifying the fear of snakes, how do you change the tone without abandoning or shelving the topic?

This is actually what speakers experience all the time—like when the audience doesn't get what you are saying, when you get a rough question from the crowd, or when someone from the audience challenges the logic of your argument.

You can't cry and walk off the stage. You can't abandon or shelve the comment. You've got to roll into it and get out of it with a meaningful redirect.

Whether it is caused by you (the speaker), limitations of the audience, or competing misinformation, the speaker has to find a way to salvage the moment. You may have to deal with it later and respond to follow-ups after, but the moment must be salvaged. The show must go on.

And to help the audience reconsider your point and redirect their attention, it is often in your interest to apply a suitable metaphor—some type of analogous relationship that will help get your point across better and faster.

After a moment to calm and collect my voice, I playfully but confidently said, "When daddy washes the car and waters the plants, what do I use?" And we got out the fact that daddy uses the water hose.

I said, "Sweetheart, if you happen to see a little snake around here, it will look something like a water hose. It'll either be wrapped up like a hose or it'll be spread out like a hose, but either way it's going to look a little bit like a water hose. Hold my hand, let's walk together, and tell each other if we see something that looks like a water hose."

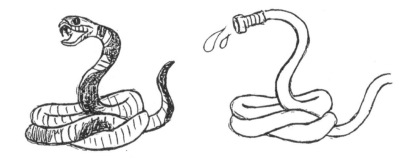

Now why do I tell you this silly story about my hiking trip a couple years ago? Because of the importance of "Mastering the Metaphor." Sometimes, when conveying information to an audience, whether it's technical or not, you will look around and see that your audience just doesn't get it, or perhaps they are challenging your ideas because of competing information.

Sometimes you can predict the confusion or challenges from your audience before you're actually on the stage. If you're being audience-centered, you'll know, or at least have a pretty good idea, of what might trip up your audience and keep them from understanding the message you're conveying.

Remember, part of your goal as a presenter is to deliver messages that are clear, concise, and compelling. Part of speaking with clarity is helping the audience grasp your message quickly, ensuring they don't work too hard to understand you or perhaps misunderstand the ideas presented.

Consider a classroom example. Imagine I was trying to explain electricity to a room of people that aren't engineers, and I were to say, "Electricity is like horse racing. The horses are the electrons, and the racetrack is the electrical circuit."

To save time as a speaker and give your audience a knowledge boost, tap into commonality—shared knowledge and understanding. My daughter and I both know what water hoses are. Most people can picture horses racing.

As a business example, imagine an alternative universe. It is the early 2000s, and you are a potential investor listening to business pitches (think of the show *Shark Tank,* and you are one of the wealthy investor-types). I walk in with a new idea and say something like, *"My idea is to develop a Facebook for working professionals. Let me explain how it will work and why this is a winning idea..."* I bet most of you, within seconds, know exactly what is being referred to...

Did you think of LinkedIn? I never had to tell you LinkedIn. And if you had never seen a LinkedIn and didn't know that one existed, you could actually start making sense of what a Facebook for working professionals might be like, and then you could decide if you like the idea or not. I don't have to draw you a picture or explain further. With only a handful of words, your mind can then wonder into a place I selected for you: a Facebook for working professionals.

Conversely, I could have spent 10 minutes trying to describe a LinkedIn, but the intent of message may get lost if the audience is all picturing very different things. Doing so might cost me loads of time that a speaker is not guaranteed. And all those pie charts and graphs can be better used during the Q/A and conversation that will ensue.

With a simple metaphor that taps into a bank of common knowledge we share. I can then ensure we are at the same starting line as I build my argument and make my case.

You know what a Facebook is, I don't have to define it for hours and elaborate with drawings. My daughter knows what a water hose is, and they don't scare her. Mastering the metaphor saves time and helps you own the message. It helps to layer your message with additional clarity, which brings us back to the main point: being speaker-centered means telling people your big idea clearly and quickly; never making your audience work hard to understand you.

Be concise

If to be clear is to make sure what you're talking about is simplified and understandable, then being concise means to make sure you are talking about the right things and only the right things.

Here is a way to think about this. Imagine you have just been asked to deliver a presentation to an audience of people younger than you. In fact, you've been asked to come speak to a room of amateurs interested in something that you know an awful lot about. Perhaps you are a great golfer speaking to people who have never held a set of clubs. Or you are a really gifted photographer speaking to a room of people who have never used an actual camera before.

In such an occasion, you are expected to be concise because, even though you know loads of information, the audience and occasion may allow you to share only a portion of what you know. So, the hard part will not be having enough to say, but knowing exactly what to share and how to share it.

You may be swimming in a sea of information, but your audience needs just a cup full.

Best in class presenters know it is their job to swim through the sea of knowledge—with their focus always on the audience and parameters of the speaking occasion—in order to develop and then deliver just the right amount of information that must be shared. This is what it means to be concise.

A great rule of thumb is:

You do not need to tell people everything you know!

In the summer of 2013, I moved back to my hometown for a tenure-track faculty position. And once there, I had the incredible opportunity to take my mom shopping for a new car. This was quite a thrill. I actually had a job, a little bit of money, and a chance to do something nice for Mom.

So, there we were at a rather nice car lot looking around at vehicles that mom might soon own and drive. And a perfectly fine salesman approaches us. Now, I'm assuming the salesman is the expert on the vehicle, not me or my mom. And I was right! He knew an awful lot about the car; so much that he was able to walk up and immediately show off all the details about the vehicle to my mom.

Think about the situation. Did he have all day to describe every detail about this vehicle to us? No, he needed to be concise. He had about a minute or less before we were going to decide whether we wanted to keep talking to him. Now, put yourself in his shoes for a moment. Given his audience (a mother and her adult son), the context (it is August in the heat of South Texas), and any other critical factors, what would you choose to focus on and point out first when making your sales pitch?

Well, you might be thinking to emphasize the air-conditioning and how the car cools down real fast by saying something like, "Go ahead. Have a seat, and let's get the air conditioning cranked up."

No, rather ironically, in that very moment, the first thing he decided to point out to my mom went something like this: "Here, have a seat. Check out how the pedals are adjustable. And right here are the seat warmers. Try that out. Look how fast that heats up!"

Then, immediately after turning on her seat warmer, he proceeds to point out an array of details about the vehicle. My mom and I did not choose that vehicle, but years later we laugh about those impressive, albeit unnecessary, seat warmers in August.

Now why would I take the time to tell you this silly story about buying a car? Because there's been an awful lot of times when I'm sitting in a presentation feeling like it's August in South Texas, and somebody chose to tell me about seat warmers.

The truth is, if you're asked to give a speech, you probably know a lot about the topic. This is a blessing that can be a burden too. With the sea of information that you are swimming in, just how will you discern what your audience must know? We live in Texas and it was the heat of August. My mom didn't need to know about the seat warmers; she needed him to turn on the air conditioning!

To be audience-centered means telling people what they must know, not all the neat and nifty things you happen to know.

That's the difference between a speaker-centered presentation versus a presenter that is audience-centered. One speaks from their perspective about what they know. The other is laser-beam focused on crafting messages that are clear and concise for the recipient.

Don't present information like kids put away clothes. Your task as a speaker is to do more than just move information from one place to another. And just because you can shove it into the dresser drawer doesn't mean you've done any real good.

...

Even when you have strong content that's clear and concise, sometimes poor structure can get in the way. **When your content is strong, but your structure is poor, it still is a failed message.**

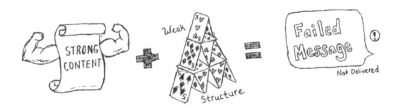

Structure smarter

The solution is to make sure you have a strong structure that will support strong content. Even if your content is clear and concise, a bad structure leaves your audience confused, if not altogether frustrated.

To illustrate the point of poor structure, I turn to an example I once read in *The Pyramid Principle* by Barbara Minto.

MEMO A:

Jim Collins telephoned to say that he can't make the meeting at 3:00. Hal Johnson says he doesn't mind making it later, or even tomorrow, but not before 10:30, and Don Clifford's secretary says that Clifford won't return from New York until tomorrow, late. The Conference Room is booked tomorrow, but free Thursday. Thursday at 11:00 looks to be a good time. Is that OK for you?

Assuming this information is all true, there is nothing *wrong* with it being said this way. But it's just weak. It's like serving someone soggy cereal. It's technically cereal, but something just isn't right with it.

This is what happens when we deliver information like a funnel—a flow of events that makes you get all the way to the end before knowing why any of it matters. By then, the main point or purpose, if even there was one, is lost somewhere in the abyss of information. Before a single bite could be enjoyed, the cereal is soggy.

This happens because the speaker/writer is taking something for granted. They take for granted that they already know the main point and purpose. So, without any consideration for their audience/reader, they decide to vomit the information chronologically because that is the natural order of events. If that same speaker/writer were to remember that they aren't talking to themselves and they're not regurgitating information that's in their head, and instead decided to give you the benefit of a main point or purpose prior to hashing events, you could chew on that information while holding that main point in mind. No soggy cereal.

So, look again at the funnel version example (i.e., Memo A) provided by Barbara Minto, where a speaker/writer rehashes information and takes their audience for granted:

MEMO A:

Jim Collins telephoned to say that he can't make the meeting at 3:00. Hal Johnson says he doesn't mind making it later, or even tomorrow, but not before 10:30, and Don Clifford's secretary says that Clifford won't return from New York until tomorrow, late. The Conference Room is booked tomorrow, but free Thursday. Thursday at 11:00 looks to be a good time. Is that OK for you?

Now, imagine what happens when the messenger takes 10 seconds to edit themselves. The revised example (i.e., MEMO B) is how to pyramid information for the benefit of the message recipient.

MEMO B:

Could we reschedule today's meeting to Thursday at 11:00? This would be more convenient for Collins and Johnson and would permit Clifford to be present.

Now, see the examples side by side:

MEMO A:	MEMO B:
Jim Collins telephoned to say that he can't make the meeting at 3:00. Hal Johnson says he doesn't mind making it later, or even tomorrow, but not before 10:30, and Don Clifford's secretary says that Clifford won't return from New York until tomorrow, late. The Conference Room is booked tomorrow, but free Thursday. Thursday at 11:00 looks to be a good time. Is that OK for you?	*Could we reschedule today's meeting to Thursday at 11:00? This would be more convenient for Collins and Johnson and would permit Clifford to be present.*

The difference between Memo A and Memo B is funneling information versus presenting as a pyramid.

FUNNELED STRUCTURE EVENTUALLY GETS TO A POINT	PYRAMID STRUCTURE BEGINS WITH THE MAIN POINT
MEMO A:	MEMO B:
Jim Collins telephoned to say that he can't make the meeting at 3:00. Hal Johnson says he doesn't mind making it later, or even tomorrow, but not before 10:30, and Don Clifford's secretary says that Clifford won't return from New York until tomorrow, late. The Conference Room is booked tomorrow, but free Thursday. Thursday at 11:00 looks to be a good time. Is that OK for you?	*Could we reschedule today's meeting to Thursday at 11:00? This would be more convenient for Collins and Johnson and would permit Clifford to be present.*

The changes from A to B in the structure, albeit subtle, and the information provided, albeit nearly identical, is conveyed in a manner that is audience-centered.

Rather than funneling tidbits of information that eventually lead to a main point, the pyramid structure begins with the main point and then provides necessary tidbits of information to help you understand and make up your mind.

That's the difference between a funnel structure and a pyramid structure. A pyramid structure of informative speaking is audience-centered and gets to the main point quickly.

Let's take it a step further, though. Applying the same concept of a pyramid, go back to the drawing board of developing and delivering a presentation. When asked to give a talk, consider that you probably weren't asked to come in and regurgitate information that someone can easily google.

So, when asked to present, ask yourself, "Why am I here? Is there a problem that we are trying to solve? A question that we are trying to answer? Some type of topic that we need new insight on?" The answer to those questions is going to make a suitable point of entry for your talk. See Example A.

EXAMPLE A: Beginning a presentation to decision-makers by using a pyramid structure and very direct introduction.

"I was invited here today to speak to you all about the concern regarding (number of slides on the playground). Given the challenges we faced (X number of kids and only X number of slides), and given some of the information that I found (currently, our kids don't like the tetherball equipment; meanwhile, playground sliding is on the rise in America), I have an approach—a possible solution—that we ought to consider (sell the existing tetherball and buy a new slide-set). For the remainder of our presentation, I will provide some additional evidence for the claims presented here, explain some additional details on how to make this happen, as well as reiterate why this is a smart solution for us. And of course, I will gladly answer your questions as they come.

In Example A, we have a solid introduction that appropriately prepares the audience for what will be presented and why. And this is critical to your effectiveness as a presenter. People are busy and multitasking. It is best to remind your audience of the purpose and the point right at the start. When they hear you speak—or even receive your memos—they don't want to work hard at understanding what you are saying, like you will see in Example B.

EXAMPLE B: Presenting without a pyramid structure and indirect introduction; speaker is merely sharing thoughts in their head.

"Good morning, everyone. As the slide says, I am Trey. And I am here to talk about what's been going on lately. Now, there is a lot to cover and there is a lot of stuff I need to update you all on. Where to begin.... Well, I've spent the past month reviewing so many important things and seeing what other people are doing. There is so much out there it would make your head spin. So, I will start from the beginning. I researched x, and learned about y. Before long, I determined that I would need to understand z. Really, I've come to learn a lot about content, content, content, content....

[nears end of presentation]

Oh, wow, I know we are running out of time here. Big picture, given all of this researching I have been doing, one solution that we might want to think about considering is (buying some more slides)."

In Example B, the audience has likely multitasked their way through a presentation that lacked clarity or structure, was not compelling, and caused them to wish they were somewhere else. At best, by the end of the presentation, the audience will think, "Oh, ok. Well, now that you've just given me that recommendation to consider, I should now go back and re-think through all of the information and data that you just presented on for 20 minutes."

Some speakers commit these presentation crimes because they don't know better. They develop and deliver their messages from a speaker-centered mindset, failing to appropriately consider and understand the mindset of their audience. Others commit these speaking crimes because they lack the confidence or assuredness required for delivering direct messages. The problem is that it becomes a self-fulfilling prophecy. The speaker lacks confidence and so delivers an unimpressive message that causes the audience to respond unfavorably, which then reinforces lack of speaker confidence.

With better structure, speakers can deliver better presentations. For starters, a better structure will mean putting key insight, main points, big takeaways, and solutions at the start of your presentation. Doing so allows the audience to focus on important information as they weigh the subsequent supporting evidence for what you are recommending, why it is the right recommendation, and how it will work.

If you follow the image below—a simple pyramid structure—you will see a visual for how a pyramid of information is presented. First, set the stage by quickly reminding the audience why you are there (e.g., on the stage, in the meeting, or in their inbox). Follow this with your big idea, perhaps the solution to the problem. Next, back the idea up by letting them know your recommendation is supported by main points, perhaps one, two, or three, each of which can have all the technical evidence and data necessary to support why it is that these main points support your big idea. And at the end, just for good measure, always bookend—the ending ought to sound similar to the beginning. That is a way to help you structure information smarter.

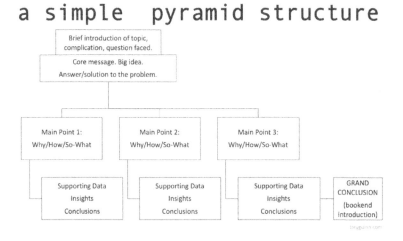

Thanks to Barbara Minto for introducing The Pyramid Structure. The Memo A and B examples that I describe come from her book, which is a helpful resource for those interested in the topic.

Be compelling

Most of the audiences I speak to can quickly identify and describe to me what the term "compelling" means and how they would use it in a sentence. Some individuals will respond that to compel is to persuade. Some will comment that a compelling argument is one that cannot be easily refuted. Think of a courtroom, where a witness provides a compelling testimony that persuades jurors toward a particular verdict.

People may be compelled by different things. Some people are compelled by logic and numbers. They believe data speaks for itself. Think of a hot topic that is debated regularly.

There are some who say, "We've got to do something about this. Look at the number of young people affected by this. The numbers don't lie. It's time we make a change."

Then there are others who are less persuaded by sheer numbers, and they say something like, "I saw the doctor talking on the news. He was in his white coat and standing in front of the hospital explaining everything. We need to listen and do something about this."

Even still, some less persuaded by spreadsheets or credibility may say something like, "I saw this interview with this beautiful kid who was upset. He was crying, and you could see it in his face that this is really affecting him and others too. Enough is enough. We've got to do something about this."

In the time of Ancient Greece, Aristotle introduced the rhetorical concepts of logos, ethos, and pathos. These three terms were used by Aristotle to help explain how rhetoric functions. When considering how compelling their argument, I encourage presenters to be sure their message has appeals to logos, ethos, and pathos.

Logos is frequently translated as some variation of logic or reasoning. In the example above, consider that some in your audience operate with the adage that numbers don't lie. To win them over, have you provided a logical argument that can be rooted in data?

Ethos is frequently translated as some variation of credibility or trustworthiness. In the example above, consider that some in your audience may only tune in and listen to a speaker who they perceive to be a trusted and credible authority figure. To win them over, have you cited your information to be associated with a trusted source? Have you found an appropriate way to give credibility and credence to the speaker (perhaps you)?

Pathos is frequently translated as some variation of emotional appeal. In the example above, consider that some in your audience may be moved by human condition and would be more persuaded by a raw testimonial account or anecdotes than bullet points and spreadsheets of numerical evidence. To win them over, have you incorporated stories and messages suited for the heart? Have you ensured that your presentation is felt, not just heard?

Now, some will mistakenly contrast pathos and logos, as if emotion and reason are mutually exclusive. So, it is worth making the point that many listeners are persuaded best when these varying appeals work in tandem. In other words, better than serving up one appeal is to incorporate and wed all three.

As you select appeals that you will use to be compelling, it is important that you remain laser-beam focused on just who you are hoping to compel. Always remember that:

Just because a message or idea compels you does not mean that it compels your audience.

To illustrate this point, consider the following:

[Knock. Knock.]

> *(Opens door) Hi, how can I help you?*

Ya, you wanna buy some magazines?

> *Um, no. Not really.*

I need to sell these magazines.
It'll help me reach my numbers.
If I reach my numbers, I'm gonna get a bonus check.

It was a decade ago, but to the best of my memory, that is verbatim my conversation with a door-to-door sales guy. I felt sorry for him. Our interaction ended with me giving him a bottled water and five dollars to get some lunch. But I had no desire to buy magazines.

According to Aristotle, where was the appeal? Did he appeal to *me* in any way? No. I suppose he provided logic about something that appealed to him (his presentation to *me* was this: if *he* reaches numbers, *he* gets a bonus check). It was a lousy speaker-centered pitch. Yet, it's a mistake any of us are capable of making.

If I had his job, I would have tried to survey everything I possibly could while approaching the home and to have quickly sized up the residents as soon as they opened the door. Had he done so, he might have tried something like:

"Hello sir. Sorry to bother you on the weekend, but I am in your neighborhood offering you and your neighbors incredible pricing on some of the world's most popular magazines. Your neighbor just ordered a year of this golf digest right here. I saw the running shoes on the steps and am guessing you might want to hear about deals on this running digest. The baby swing out front tells me you might also be interested in this parenting periodical. Again, I don't mean to take too much time, but would you give me just one minute so I can tell you about our best-in-class reputation and unbeatable pricing?"

I can't promise that my revised approach would have worked, but the audience-centered style would have been far more impressive and would have caused more people to hear him out.

Remember: you have a goal, but you don't decide if you reach your goal; the audience does. Just because an idea compels you does not mean it compels your audience.

The odds of compelling the listener are in your favor when you utilize Aristotle's appeals and keep your focus on your audience.

Your ideas won't appeal to everyone. In fact, many people are bombarded with ideas, and so they are immediately turned off at the thought of another one.

For this reason, I urge you to not begin an email, call, or presentation with the phrase, "I have an idea that I want to share." The magazine salesman had an idea: "If you buy some magazines it will help me reach my numbers."

Whether we realize it or not, a lot of our communication can sound this way. Take, for instance, the student who tells his professor, "I need an A in this class to keep my scholarship." This may be a very compelling argument to the student, but how is this supposed to compel the professor?

How would you advise a student in this situation to rethink their approach and messaging?

I'd advise him to consider that the speaker-centered nature of "I need an A to keep my scholarship," is about as compelling to a professor as it was for me to hear a salesman say, "I need to sell magazines." Duh. I know that you need to sell magazines. I know that you want to get an A.

Don't tell me the idea that is important to you. Help me understand the problem, how it impacts me, and how you propose to solve it.

"Professor, my grades aren't where they should be. This is a problem, as I depend on my scholarship to be a student here. I know that I can do better, and I'm willing to do the work. I have a solution that I'd like to discuss with you."

Again, I won't promise that this style of messaging will work every time, but being audience-centered is far more likely to cause the listener to hear with an open-mind. At minimum, it is far more promising of an approach than merely saying, "I really need an A in this class to keep my scholarship."

A lot of times, decision makers (the people who will be in your audience, especially when you go out into the workforce) aren't interested in your ideas. They've got ideas piled up high all over their desk. But, you know what they need? They need people who can spot and solve pre-existing problems. So, I dare you to take your next nifty idea and repackage it as a solution to a pre-existing problem. If you don't remind your audience of the problem being solved and the pain being alleviated by your solution, your grand thought and big idea is all too easy to ignore, delete, or just leave on the dusty bookshelf of forgotten ideas.

Imagine your audience has a big headache. To walk in declaring your big ideas, unaware of their pain, is potentially adding to the inflammation. Conversely, to be audience-centered would mean discovering how your idea and presentation can be the ibuprofen to their headache.

Let's tie some of this together. You want strong content plus strong structure to support it. You aren't wondering what you think of the message or even what a previous audience would think of a message; instead, you are laser-beam focused on this audience and how they will receive that message.

It's never a love letter, "to whom it may concern." You're speaking to real humans and they're asking themselves, "What's in this for me?" If developing content and structure with audience in mind, you are well on your way to a winning presentation.

Next, is ensuring that you are presenting with confidence, both verbally and nonverbally. There are some clear markers of confidence portrayed verbally. One, as we mentioned before, is to declare the big idea quickly and clearly. This signals to the audience that you are not hiding, but instead you are highlighting the main point. A bold, confident move.

Second, as the speaker, you want to anticipate and appropriately refute probable resistance. One of the key things in being an audience-centered speaker is to anticipate what about your message they may potentially reject. In other words, what will be the rebuttal to you and what you are sharing? There are actually some really important strategies for working probable rebuttals into your presentation.

Where some presenters try to run from the resistance and play ignorant to the probable obstacles they will face from the audience, I highly advise that they instead run through the resistance with well-timed refutation strategies. Often, it serves you better to refute rebuttals during your presentation, and to avoid having to address them awkwardly during a question and answer period.

How does a refutation strategy work?

Entire bookshelves could be filled with all that has been written and said about doing and mastering a refutation strategy. Let me paint a simple picture for you in hopes to sum up a few ideas. Imagine you work for the American Red Cross and you've walked into a college classroom with the goal of recruiting people to donate blood and time to your organization.

You could give them a standard introduction on who the Red Cross is, what you do, and why it matters, etc. And then you better get to the point where you ask the audience for what you want. Chances are the audience will feel encouraged to hear the good you are doing...until you ask them to donate their own blood and time. That is the point when their brains start going, "No way, I don't do needles," or "Wish I could help, but I don't have time. I am way too stressed about this midterm next week."

You, the speaker, should always be able to anticipate the rebuttal from the audience. Some speakers sadly don't care enough about their audience to think of the probable rebuttal; others fear their audience and the possible rebuttal, and so hide from both.

Your best option is to tackle the most likely rebuttals head on. Just after you ask them to donate their blood and time, you should pause, and with honest eyes, a kind and confident smile, and say something like:

"Now, I understand some people in this room might be scared of needles. I don't want you to be. In fact, in my experience I have seen that even when people are nervous about giving blood, they manage to have a good time at the donation station when they bring a friend and do it together. Or, if your friend can't be there, find me, and I will be your friend. I'll even hold your hand if you want!"

Then, pause again and say something like:

"But if that doesn't work for you, or if for some health reason you aren't able to give blood, I want you to know there are other ways to donate—like with your time. We need good people like you to help us set up the booths, greet people as they arrive, and thank them when they leave. Now, if you are like me when I was in college, you might not find yourself with a lot of free time to donate. I am here to tell you that even one hour a month makes a huge difference, not just for us but also for you. Donating time to a worthy cause can lift your mood and make you feel proud. Most of our volunteers come back and end up donating more time month after month because they find that the experience of helping with our organization boosts their mood and helps them take their mind off the stress of college. So, think of it not just as an hour given but a sense of purpose gained."

Of course, I could keep going with examples and drown the presentation in refutation, but it would be overkill. A strong refutation does not have to be five times the size of the rebuttal. To over refute is to oversell, and then your audience feels like you are being insincere or calculated.

Third, while you want to slay your hardest probable questions during your presentation by using well-placed refutation strategies, you do still want to warmly welcome the question and answer period. It is one of the most critical things you can do as you close your presentation.

Many people will try to avoid Q&A or may welcome it half-heartedly with something like: "We might have time for a question if there is one out there, but I don't see any hands up. So, I think we are good. Ok, thanks again for your time. Bye." Some don't sound scared of Q&A, but still offer up a poor attempt with, "Ok, are there any questions?" This is not necessarily bad, but it's not your best option. Remember that this is the end of your presentation, your parting moments with your audience. If a presentation is like dinner with a friend, think of the question and answer time like when you get up from the table and begin to say goodbye.

Make the question and answer time a chance to demonstrate warmth and ensure a positive and lasting impact on your time together. Don't weakly call for questions and then walk off, just like you wouldn't finish dinner and then rush out the door awkwardly or deny the hug.

Calling for questions is your time to seal the deal with a warm smile, kind word, and goodbye hug. Anticipate there will be questions, and in most cases, when you set a warm, inviting tone, your audience will do the same when asking their questions. Set the right tone with something like, "Thank you all so much for allowing me the pleasure of presenting here today. I certainly hope to keep the conversation going well after this event, but for now, what questions do you have for me?"

These are just a few of the ways we can project confidence through verbal communication choices. In the chapter to follow, we will begin exploring some of the ways we demonstrate confidence nonverbally.

TREY GUINN

CHAPTER 8

DELIVERY:
DON'T JUST SING THE SONG,
SELL IT.

I am a lucky dad. Aside from travel or late appointments, my work schedule has enough flexibility that I get to spend a lot of time with my kids before and after school and through much of the summer. With all of that time together, we develop some pretty goofy games and rituals. One is to put the windows down and sing along to the radio as loud as we want. Last summer, we were cruising home from a trip to a favorite neighborhood playground, when my oldest daughter picked the next song—*I'm Still Standing* by Elton John. She was starting to get into it, when low and behold, we pulled up to a streetlight, and the car beside us was a family we knew well.

Joy said, "Turn it up, and put my window down." It was clear to me she wanted to go full-blown Carpool Karaoke for this one. As I am putting the window down, her little sister slaps her on the arm and reminds her, "Don't just sing it. You gotta sell it, Joy!" She was seven years old, but understood quite well that there is an art, a finesse, to delivery. You can't just sing it, say it, or write it. You've gotta sell it!

And she did. Within milliseconds, Joy threw on some oversized sunglasses and grabbed the hairbrush-microphone from the seat pocket in front of her.

She transformed herself into a mini Elton John but with moves like Jagger. She didn't just sing the song. She sold it.

Our friends in the car next to us watched with jaws dropped. In seconds, the mom was shaking her head and laughed momentarily, just before we both drove our separate ways. That was all. It was the appropriate reaction to her performance.

Notice: I didn't say they jumped out of the car and started dancing in the streets. They merely paused with a bit of awe and had a momentary laugh. Had my daughter undersold it with the window up and just a hairbrush to her lips, they may have looked over with curiosity, and perhaps even assumed that she was unaware she was on display. If she had oversold it by pulling on her hair while screaming the song and kicking out a glass window, they may have called the police.

Joy, just like a presenter on the stage, had to first discern what response she sought to elicit from her audience. From there, she knew how to deliver the performance necessary to achieve her goal—a sincere, albeit momentary, laugh.

And that is what should drive delivery. Not that we always mimic one person or style, but that we be forward-thinking and equally nimble in knowing our desired audience perception and response at a given moment. We should always be asking:

What do I want them to think of me and my message? How do I want them to respond?

Sure, the message, the very words, ought to have an impact of their own. And we know this can be true, as often we are moved by merely reading a story, a speech, or lines from a play. But to elicit the greatest response from our audience, there is a whole world of vocal and visual delivery skills available to us. And we ought to master them as best we are able. By doing so, we don't just sing our song. We sell it.

The truth about competence & confidence

I get alarmed when a new client books time with me solely to write a speech or *develop* a presentation but has no interest in rehearsing the *delivery*. Yes, the words you say matter. So do visual aids, like a slide deck. It all matters. But too many people overemphasize the development of a speech at the peril of delivering it well.

I hear rationales like, "There isn't time to rehearse it. I just need to get the deck put together and make sure the information looks right," or, "Thanks for writing this. I am sure it's great. I am going to give it a couple reads in the morning and should be good to go!" Technically, that is their choice and not mine. But it would be malpractice for me to take the money and run.

At minimum, I always insist on building in time to do a few run throughs of the talk as we go. The speaker has to get a feel for the timing and flow of a talk. They need to make sure they feel good about their vocal delivery and that the visual delivery is strong, not awkward.

Almost always, by the end of the first and even second run through, it is obvious to the speaker and me that delivery is lacking, and developing great content won't be enough. But even still, sometimes a client is ok with that and assumes the delivery doesn't matter. They'd rather be sure the words are perfect, because they just can't afford to say the wrong thing and blow their credibility.

Here is where I get even more concerned. Yes, it's a fair point that a speaker should nail the content and edit the message to be as accurate and on-point as possible. But to assume that credibility is earned or lost by the words alone naively underestimates how much of credibility is dependent on audience perception, a byproduct not just of the actual content, but also (and often more so) the speaker's delivery.

Let me reiterate, I am not arguing that we don't need to be precise with content, especially critical data, financials, medical information, etc. I am also not suggesting foregoing accuracy of information and jumping to rehearsal. Instead, I am insisting speakers make time for both.

Consider the argument made earlier about speaker credibility. It is one of the primary appeals taught to us by Aristotle. We know audiences are persuaded by speakers who demonstrate credibility. Speakers incorporate credibility into their message content by referencing their own experience. They can lean on credibility from outside sources (like a reputable study or example). Audience-centered presenters can capitalize on speaker credibility by establishing how a topic is relevant to the audience, which demonstrates shared values between audience and speaker.

In terms of delivery, however, speakers are perceived as credible when they speak confidently and authentically. And it is important to do so, because we know audiences are more likely to stay focused on the content, and are even more likely to be persuaded, if they believe the speaker stands behind their message.

Picture a time you have seen a presenter shrug their shoulders and say, "This seems kind of important because the book talked about it," or with an uptick in their voice said, "This seems like something we maybe should consider." The words don't sell the credibility of the claims, but perhaps even worse is that the visual shoulder shrug and vocal uptick confirm to the audience that the speaker is unenthusiastic and might not even agree with or care about what they are saying. And if that is the case, why should the audience care?

In the mind of the audience, speaker credibility is out the window, and the time given listening to this presentation is utterly wasted.

When speakers use tentative or vague language, or their visual and vocal delivery skills look and sound timid, the audience is more likely to question the speaker's credibility or the authenticity in what they're saying. Therefore, it is imperative speakers are sharp both in what they say and how they say it.

A little secret about establishing credibility

Think for a minute about who is often asked to be the presenter. Do you frequently see an amateur speaking to a room of experts? No. Of course not. More often than not, the speaker is an expert speaking to a room of people who know less, and perhaps even care less, about the topic that the speaker is presenting about. It is normal for a speaker to be more knowledgeable about and invested in a topic than the audience she or he is speaking to.

Given that, what is the most logical way for an audience to discern credibility of the speaker? The confidence the speaker portrays. Don't believe me? Watch the news or a live sporting event. Check out a political debate. Who is winning on-air: someone who speaks with the accuracy of an encyclopedia but seems to have shaky and underdeveloped confidence, or someone who has unflappable confidence, and from the best you can tell, knows what they are talking about?

I wish for you to develop both the competence and confidence necessary to win over your audiences. But never overlook the importance of gaining credibility from the very start and throughout the entire message, by simply demonstrating the vocal and visual delivery skills that project confidence.

Most of the individuals I work with understand that competence is harder to prove than confidence, and therefore, audiences are more quickly persuaded by confidence than competence. This is because if you are on the stage, the assumption is that you know what you are talking about. But in about 20 seconds, the audience is going to know if you are comfortable up there and capable of delivering your message with confidence.

Right now, as I write this chapter, my phone is getting a notification every five minutes about COVID-19 (the coronavirus). This is universally true. It seems across the globe that people everywhere are social-distancing, staying home, and collecting information about the virus from numerous sources—political leaders, medical professionals, and media personalities alike.

If I learn that an infectious disease doctor is about to give a press conference about the disease on television, I, like so many around the country, would turn on the TV to see the doctor speak. I am not a medical doctor (so I am less knowledgeable), but I am a concerned citizen (so I am invested in the topic); however, this infectious disease doctor presumably knows a lot about the topic and is even more invested in the situation than me and all those tuning in.

As an audience member, is it easy for me to know if what he says is accurate? I suppose I could google every word he says to see if he is textbook accurate, and perhaps I could call other doctor friends of mine to get their opinions on what he is saying, but chances are I don't have the kind of time to fact check the speaker as they speak. So then, how will I make sense of how credible he is as a speaker?

Rather than fact check him, I can listen to the tone of the speaker and observe his actual style. I can get a sense of his vibe and the amount of confidence he appropriately projects. And from all those nonverbal indicators, I will begin to discern my own perception of him.

Unable to determine whether he is more competent than most, as an audience member, I will begin to make sense of how confident he appears while speaking. His own projection of confidence will then inevitably shape my perceptions of his competence and the message he is delivering.

My perception of his confidence will shape my perception of his competence. And this is what happens in most presentations. We get a sense of speaker confidence before ever being able to discern speaker competence. If credibility is established through a blend of speaker competence and confidence, yet it is easier for the audience to determine your confidence than your competence, which of the two is a must have?

The answer is easy: confidence. Unless you are speaking before a hostile group, most audiences want you to succeed. It's painful to watch a speaker stumble and bumble their way through a talk. When a speaker doesn't already have well-known, established credibility, confidence is the foundation for other audience perceptions to build upon.

What exactly do confident speakers do?

With regard to verbal communication (words) and decisions related to message content, confident speakers use assuring and descriptive language. But even more than this, they are intentional with all the nonverbal elements. They have good posture, use purposeful movement, use open gestures, and make eye contact. A speaker with a commanding presence and good posture appears more confident than a speaker who appears to shrink by slouching.

Conversely, audiences perceive a speaker to have low confidence when using extreme eye contact behavior (e.g., very little or staring in one spot). As well, those who fail to move or place themselves as far from the audience as possible are seen as less confident.

To strengthen vocal quality, confident speakers stand erect and breathe from their stomach rather than their chest. Perhaps you are like many people, students, and clients that I work with and find yourself struggling to project a confident voice. You are just fine all day, and then, right before taking the stage, your vocal cords tighten, and you struggle to have a strong presentation voice.

One of the best ways I know how to help people overcome this struggle—and the struggle is real— is by helping them picture that it is not a presentation at all, but instead it is merely a conversation with a friend.

Take the stage, find the friendly faces in the room, and begin to imagine your presentation is merely a story you are telling those friendly faces over a cup of coffee.

More about strengthening vocal delivery

Your vocal delivery as a presenter is comprised of many things, some which may seem common knowledge and others not so much. As a speaker, audiences are evaluating your articulation, fillers, pitch, rate, timbre, tone and emotion, and use of pauses. They may not know they are doing it, but somehow each of these vocal qualities are informing their overall perception of you.

For instance, audiences evaluate your articulation when they make sense of how well you form and utter the words that come out of your mouth; they may say something like, "She speaks really clearly. I like that I can understand her very easily." If the way you form and utter words makes an unclear sound and hinders an audience's ability to understand you, they may deem you as inarticulate or even unconfident, driving them to perceive you and your message poorly.

Filler words

Many people comment to me that—umm, like, you know—the wish they could stop saying filler words (aka, verbal disfluencies). Vocal fillers are sounds and words that fill silence and do not add to the content of a message (e.g., 'uh,' 'um,' 'like,' etc.). When used with high frequency, filler words hinder speaker's message clarity and are distracting to the audience.

Vocal fillers influence the audience's perceptions of a speaker's credibility, preparedness, and confidence—if you speak with too many fillers, people will be likely to perceive you as not credible, unprepared, and even insecure. Because filtering out all those fillers requires more cognitive effort, audiences are quick to tune out disfluent speakers in favor of an easier task such as thinking of their to-do lists.

While some of my clients come to me hoping to completely eliminate all filler words, I remind them that this may not be the right goal. Truth is, unless you are giving a State of the Union type of presentation, most audiences expect an occasional disfluency—it makes you sound human, giving a conversational vibe to your speaking.

Used sparingly and effectively, filler words can make you more relatable to your audience, give you time to catch your breath, and emphasize key points. But when they become crutch words used out of nervousness or lack of preparation, they diminish your credibility.

If you recognize a word you overuse, such as "like" or starting sentences with "you know," you can begin training yourself to reduce your use. I had a friend who wore a rubber band on his wrist and would snap it every time he had a disfluency. Apparently, it was effective, but I'd like to think you can discover a less painful way to break your vocal habits. When on the stage, the best way to eliminate them is to slow your rate of speech and master the art of the pause.

Pauses

Pauses, however, aren't easy to embrace. Many presenters feel like even the briefest pause can feel like forever. But it usually only feels that way to the one on the stage.

If you demonstrate assuredness as you pause, the audience will give you the benefit of the doubt and determine that your pause is intentional. So, take your pause and own it.

When speakers choose to press the pause button on their own mouths, the benefits are a plenty. Pausing allows you to collect your thoughts and get back on track. The best way to use them is when building suspense.

A strategically placed silence can build suspense, emphasize a point, or give the audience time to absorb a key insight. I pause regularly through a presentation. It gives me a second to breathe and re-engages my audience. And I build them into my presentations to be and feel organic, as part of the talk.

> **"Pausing is an important skill for public speakers.**
> *(pause; look out to the audience with wonder)*
> **And imagine why that might be.**
> *(pause; look up/off and then back at your audience)*
> **Perhaps it is because..."**

Like filler words, pauses give you a chance to take a break and figure out what comes next. However, a pause makes you sound confident and in control, whereas overused filler words are distracting and make you sound as if you don't know what to say. A well-timed pause may also play to the emotion in the room, as it causes the audience to sit with a thought and reflect on what has been said or what they anticipate hearing next.

Tone and emotion

An engaging vocal delivery helps speakers to connect with their audiences and can be used to highlight key concepts a presenter wishes for the listener to cue in on.

A presenter's tone and emotion does more than just captivate the listener and increase the likelihood a presentation will be remembered fondly.

In fact, tone and emotion strengthens the likelihood the message be remembered at all. Meaning, when speakers can elicit an emotional response from the audience, the audience is more likely to remember the message itself. This seems like a no-brainer, but it is incredibly important to remember as a presenter.

If you care about your message and want your audience to care too, then at minimum, increase your tone and emotion, as it will drive the likelihood your audience will remember, perhaps ruminate on, what you shared. While of course you can inject your voice with exaggerated tone and emotion when the moment calls for it, your default mode as a presenter should be to speak with a warm and inviting voice, as though you have just opened the doors of your home to friends and neighbors.

Following the metaphor, just as you'd guide first-time visitors on a warm and inviting tour of your home, so too you would guide your audience with a warm, inviting, and conversational tone from the start through the finish of your presentation. Warm tone and emotion increase the likelihood that the audience will relate to the speaker; audiences tend to like people they can relate with.

From vocal to visual delivery

While vocal and visual elements of delivery are distinct, they work best in tandem. Meaning, whatever you are doing visually should be intentionally aligned with whatever you are doing vocally. Unless for a specific purpose like irony or humor, effective speakers match tone and emotion to their facial expressions to help clarify and support the intended message.

Likewise, a speaker's tone and emotion are better understood when gestures are used to support and clarify the message. This seems so obvious, as we learn from a young age to match our words with our voice and our gestures. A person who is giddy to see a loved one may raise the pitch of their voice and throw open their arms as they say, "I've missed you! Get over here and give me a hug!" You can imagine how weird it would be to hear someone say those words with a high-pitched voice, yet their body is slouched and closed off.

I can't keep count of all the times I see presenters make claims and announcements to an audience while slouched from behind a lectern. Many presenters will explain it away as, "I just don't know what to do with my hands up there." Perhaps a bit harshly, I ask something like, "You've had them your whole life. What have you been doing with them?" It's as if once a person gets on stage, they forget how to align themselves such that their words match their vocal and visual delivery.

Even when we get past the hurdle of not knowing what to do with our hands and feet on stage, there are still things that savvy presenters must watch out for. I've worked with financial leaders preparing earnings reports, and when we begin rehearsing a presentation intended to calm the audience with words like "all in all, things are looking up" or "profits are on the rise," I find they are pushing their hands in a downward motion as they say it.

Here is where quality rehearsal and being mindful of all the details of your presentation can make the difference, especially when we know people listen more for what you do than what you say. I started the chapter urging you to not just sing the song; instead, you gotta sell it. One way to sell the message is to ensure your vocal and visual delivery are coordinated with and enhancing your message, never betraying it!

The eyes have it!

Eye contact is an incredibly powerful tool to connect with other people. Plenty has been written about the cultural cues a presenter should be mindful of when considering giving and receiving eye contact. Most agree that Western culture places a premium on eye contact, with perception being that people who give too little eye contact are either impolite, insecure, or perhaps even untrustworthy. While staring or giving creepy eye contact is intimidating, awkward, and may even appear threatening, appropriately strong eye contact leads audiences to like the presenter more.

The expectations for eye contact during one-on-one conversation remain mostly true for presentations to small and large groups. The caveat is the presenter should not expect to receive eye contact, but instead must give great eye contact and hope the eye contact modeled is reciprocated by the audience.

Savvy speakers aim to make eye contact with each person in the room, and many will work the room with their eyes by going from one side to the other or making natural z-type patterns with their eyes. That said, it would be unnatural and very awkward to meet eyes with each person down the row, handing each person a moment of eye contact like you were passing out candy.

Solid eye contact is about three seconds and not much longer. Eye contact with any individual should not last longer than the duration of a phrase or thought. This amount of eye contact allows for a meaningful connect with an individual without making any audience member feel singled out. This also allows you, the speaker, to get a sense of how your audience members are receiving and reacting to you message.

All eyes on me

In 1995 Tupac Shakur released a hit album entitled *All Eyez on Me*, which received its name because the artist felt like no matter where he went or what he did that all eyes—police, jealous rappers, feds, women, and more—were on him. That was 1995, and I'd argue that, a quarter-century since then, eye contact in our society has diminished. Perhaps I should clarify. All eyes on screens has increased; human eye contact has suffered.

Even in the past ten years, I've seen that the struggle for solid eye contact is real. Clients of all ages report to me the challenges they face getting comfortable looking at the audience in the eye, even when the audience is one person during a face-to-face job interview.

Hear me loud and clear, unlike many of my contemporaries, I actually don't blame young people; they're growing up with parents glued to their phones and adults that check emails while talking to their family members.

My heart breaks when I see a kid holler something like, "Dad, watch me do this cannonball!" and I see the dad make a thumbs-up and respond, "Great job!" all while staring at his phone. All eyes on screen. Yuck!

And worse, I commit the same error sometimes. During family dinner, my pocket buzzes, and I feel that urge to check my phone while still part of the conversation. Not only are adults trading eye contact for screen time, but our poor behavior-modeling is teaching young people that eye contact is unimportant.

For these reasons, I am not surprised when I get funny looks from students and clients when I demand they strengthen their eye contact. It's like I've just asked them to write a sentence in cursive. *Write the sentence...why wouldn't I just type it? Write it in cursive... who even does that anymore?*

But when I explain to my clients why it matters so much,

they begin to get it and ask, "How can I improve?" This is because somewhere inside of us we know how good it feels to be seen and how much we appreciate eye contact that is warm, inviting, kind, and displays confidence and sincerity.

Eye contact is like a lost art. The rarer it becomes, the more precious it will become. Those who do it well will continue to be seen as those leaders amongst us who have the "it" factor; a certain magnetism we crave and almost miss.

Good news, growing your eye contact skills is simple.

Eye contact is like a muscle. If you grow it, it will be there and ready for you when you need it.

If you don't grow it, you can't expect to have it for use. Imagine spending your life without ever lifting a thing and then walking into the gym and reaching for the 100-pound dumbbells, expecting to rep heavy weight. Not going to happen.

But the person who goes to the gym and reps the lighter weights will see progress in time; with commitment to lifting, they will soon be reaching for heavier and heavier weights. Before long, they will have grown the muscles needed for lifting those heavy weights.

Your eye contact muscles work similarly. If you avoid and ignore eye contact with others regularly and tend to spend your days *all eyes on screen*, attempting to give a presentation with *eyes on your audience* will seem impossible. Committing your eyes to your audience through the duration of a speech is heavy weight, intended only for those with strong eye contact muscles.

Like someone developing their arm muscles by lifting lighter weights at the start and then going up in weight, you do the same for your eye contact skills. You start by treating each human interaction as a chance to grow eye contact muscles. Wave, smile, and make eye contact with the person crossing the street. Give eye contact and say a friendly hello to the person passing you in the grocery store. Make small talk with strong eye contact with your barista next time you order a coffee.

If you practice eye contact in low-stake interactions, the muscles will grow and be readily available in time for the high-stake interactions. I mean really, if 60 seconds of eye contact with the barista seems uncomfortable, how does eye contact throughout a 45-minute interview or 20-minute presentation sound?

I have said much already about how audiences perceive the confidence of their speaker. I have focused on vocal and visual delivery, like filler words, pausing, hand gestures, and even eye contact. But the reality is that your audience has likely already evaluated your confidence well before then.

Confidence is perceived well before the presenter speaks.

I was in the fifth grade, and I had been invited to a birthday party. This was not any birthday party. This was the birthday party of my grade-school crush. This was a big deal!

Saturday afternoon came, and I was ready. My mom dropped me off at the house 15 minutes after the start time—she had convinced me that arriving casually late was a cool thing. I waved bye to mom and walked toward the house with a gift in hand. The birthday girl's mom opened the door and let me in. I peeked around and saw no one.

The mom walked me through to the kitchen. I asked where to put the gift and inquired about where everyone was. She took the gift and very politely showed me to the back door. With all the eagerness of a kid in a candy store, I opened the back door. And in a moment, my eyes bugged out and my jaw dropped. I was aghast and quickly stepped back inside. I shut the door. I found a guest bathroom, locked the door, and tried to control my anxiety.

Why didn't I know this was a pool party? Everyone was swimming and playing, and I didn't have my swimsuit. Even worse, the other fifth grade boys looked like Greek gods out there, bouncing beach balls and squirting water guns like they belonged in a swimwear catalog of cool kids.

I felt like a total dork, and I wasn't even dressed to swim! And this wasn't just any party. It was my crush's house and the party of the year.

What on earth was I going to do? Should I run for the front door and try to chase down my mom's car to avoid the party altogether? Or would it be better to hang back in the kitchen, pretend to be helpful by frosting the cupcakes?

I don't know how, but in my gut I knew this was a life moment, a make or break opportunity. I dug deep and called upon all the confidence I could muster. I took a good look in the mirror before dropping to the floor in the bathroom and doing the wimpiest two pushups you could ever see.

I pumped my chest a little, made my way for the back. I swung open the door, threw on a smile, and as I headed toward the pool, locked eyes with the birthday girl, waved to my friends, declared "cannonball!" and jumped right in!

I was scared, but I stepped up. Something in me knew I would not be able to walk out there cold, feeling like a loser, and expecting myself to warm up into feeling like a winner. Focusing on discomfort doesn't somehow generate feelings of comfort. Likewise, I wasn't going to limp over to the pool timidly with my head down to find a pool full of people telling me how great I was and how excited they were to see me.

If I wanted to feel confident and earn attention from my peers and crush, I was going to have to dig deep, find confidence within, and project that confidence outwardly.

I think many speakers face similar situations. A presentation might intimidate them, but by the week of, they may be feeling good about it. They may look forward to it even, as I did that birthday party. Then, before they take the stage, something inside freaks them out a bit, like when I looked out and saw the cool kids splashing around and having fun.

Some scared speakers will call in sick or ask someone else to give the presentation. Others show up reluctantly and deliver nervously. Either way, audiences can smell fear and spot a scared presenter a mile away. Not really, but audiences size up a speaker the moment they enter the room.

"He looks young. And is he sweating?"

> "He is well-dressed. He carries himself well and seems friendly."

"She looks nervous. Why is she pacing the room?"

> "Oh, she looks really put together and seems like a nice person."

"Oh, great. He can't seem to figure out the projector. This presentation is off to a great start."

Indeed, evaluative thoughts about you are being made before you ever open your mouth. Since we know that, work it to your advantage. Get your game face on before you even enter the building. Start projecting your best self well before start time. Unless inappropriate for the occasion, smile like you've just been given a promotion. If you move, do so with pep in your step. Don't stare at your notes and phone; instead, give eye contact generously to the speaker before you and/or the people in the room. All those little things are combining to give the audience a sense of your visual presence. Your visual presence is fueling their perception of you as either being a confident (and *ipso facto* competent) presenter—all before you ever take the stage and open your mouth.

TREY GUINN

PART 3

THE WRAP UP SIGNAL

CHAPTER 9

IN CONCLUSION

When I started writing this book, I was sitting in my hotel suite in Savannah, Georgia. I had just finished delivering a presentation to a very warm and receptive crowd who showed every indication they appreciated me being there. They stood, clapped, and even stayed around asking me to sign copies of my book, *Adventures in Adulting.*

I left the presentation feeling the perfect balance of being depleted (because I left all I had on the stage) and high on life (because I knew I had nailed it). The goal of my presentation was met, and the audience perception of me was strong and positive. Those feelings of success are what motivated me to write this book for you, my students, clients, audiences, and readers everywhere.

My goal in writing this book is to help more people experience the sense of accomplishment and personal satisfaction that comes from enhancing presentational effectiveness.

When it comes to human communication and public speaking, the struggle is real; the message sent is not always the message received. This problem is magnified in light of the fact that many people lack the willingness to present and readiness to do so effectively. You can be different. You can do better.

With the right **mindset**, a willingness to try, learn, and grow, you can develop the readiness to be a best-in-class presenter. If you adopt **Trey's Triangle**, you will be a speaker who can adapt your **message** and **delivery** for your **audience** in order to accomplish your **goals**.

Like juggling, thinking through Trey's Triangle may seem an unnatural task at first, but the more you do it, the simpler it will become, the smoother your communication process will be, and the more variables you'll learn to juggle at once.

Confident vocal and visual delivery should become second nature for you. Developing *audience-centered messages that are clear, concise, and compelling* should be standard for every note you send and time you speak.

That is the core message of this book. And that is precisely what I have wanted to share with you since I was sitting in my hotel suite in Savannah, Georgia.

But that was one month ago. Today, sitting in the front room of my home, enjoying a coffee, looking out a large window that stares into the front yard, I am again feeling inspired to write. Specifically, I've decided to rewrite this conclusion chapter.

Like a presenter who tears up his speaking notes mid-presentation and decides to go impromptu, I am here deleting the original conclusion in favor of typing this one now. Much global unrest and our current climate have reminded me to use these pages to reemphasize a critical point that has been mentioned before but bears repeating – **be nimble.**

Presentations are dynamic; therefore, effectiveness requires you to be nimble!

You see, as I attempt to get a single word onto the page, my phone is being pinged mercilessly. It is March of 2020, and the evolving coronavirus pandemic is top of mind for everyone. In addition to news alerts and messaging with family and friends, event organizers and points of contact are pinging me about upcoming work.

Ultimately, in light of coronavirus and social distancing, anything face-to-face is being cancelled, rescheduled, or changed to a virtual format. For the meetings, talks, and workshops still happening, there are now a number of new things that I (the speaker) must consider. The presentation plans I had prepared and developed are now thrown out the window, and everything must be re-evaluated in light of the change of format for delivery.

First, I can assume my audiences, like people all over the world, will be rightly focused on this virus and how it is impacting them personally and professionally. To stick to a prepared script and not adapt the message accordingly would be foolish. This means that all presentations will undergo much more development and preparation to ensure my content shows understanding of and sensitivity to the way people are thinking and feeling in light of this pandemic.

It is also an opportunity for me to rethink the examples and metaphors I use, ensuring I am able to maximize the moment and illustrate key points using current events.

While adapting your presentation to the state of a pandemic is unlikely, changes in format or environment are common and require you be nimble. Knowing that most of my foreseeable talks for the remainder of 2020 will be webinars, I will be kept on my toes. A webinar where I share my screen and talk for an hour or more without any verbal feedback from an audience, who is likely sipping coffee and multitasking from their home office, is far different than being with those same people live all in one space, where I am able to present interactively and engage my audience with activities.

Alas, the move from a live event to a webinar is something I am familiar with. On many occasions, a firm will change the format for any number of reasons. *"We've invited global partners to join, so it will be better for us to film you and stream it,"* or, *"The team won't be at the home office. They are all on client sites, so we are going to do a webinar instead. And rather than two hours, this will need to be 45-minutes."*

I am used to getting format changes, sometimes even the day of the event, even after I have already flown into the city where I was supposed to present live. Smaller changes to the format and environment are almost a given. *"Hey, our tech people can't get the [insert name of technology here] working. Are you still good to go?"* My first thought tends to be something like, "You want me to facilitate a four-hour workshop for 150+ people without a microphone or projector for my slide deck? And you are telling me this right now, when I am supposed to begin the session in 10-minutes?" My answer is always something like, "You got it. I was born ready!" What benefit is gained by complaining or signaling that I can't get the job done?

If I have committed to the presentation, I am not going to walk away, which means I will be presenting. If I am presenting, failure isn't an option. So, once I have assured the organizer everything will be just fine, I take a moment to revisit the basics.

In other words, any curveball is no problem at all. Whatever problem arises, the answer is to revisit Trey's Triangle. What is my goal? Who is my audience? Given any new information and complications, how should I be nimble and adjust my message content and delivery? If you can keep a laser-beam focus on those core things, you will be well on your way toward enhancing presentational effectiveness.

Thank you so much for reading. This book has been an absolute pleasure to write! I hope you will stay connected with me at treyguinn.com.

Wishing you and yours all the very best!

Trey

CHAPTER 10

WHAT QUESTIONS DO YOU HAVE FOR ME

*This bonus chapter is still in progress and under-development. Enjoy what is here and check back for more soon!

Which matters more: what you say or how you say it?

I get this question regularly. And it is always portrayed as an either/or proposition. Like when you hear a couple fighting and someone will say, "It's not what you said, it's how you said it." When it comes to public speaking though, audience perception is usually not rooted in either/or; instead, the audience expects you to be wonderful in both.

A frequent criticism about *what* people say has to do with message *clarity*, which we established earlier to be the evaluation of a speaker's chosen words, phrases, and sentences. The easier it is for the audience to understand a speaker's vocabulary, grammar, and style, the more credible they deem the speaker to be. To expand on that, imagine you've got your message nice and clear, but now it becomes about how you say it.

One common area of critique in regard to how a message is communicated comes down to a speaker's *pitch variation,* which is how effectively a speaker varies the high and low intonation of their voice. Patterns in pitch can negatively impact an audience's perception of credibility. For example, when a speaker ends every sentence with an upward pitch inflection, audiences perceive the speaker to be less credible. This is in part because this inflection sounds like a question, implying that the person making the statement is unsure.

CHAPTER 11

ENCORE:
ADVENTURES IN PUBLIC SPEAKING

This is a developing and growing feature of the book. The more stories acquired and shared, the more will be posted in future editions. With that, we'd love to help you tell your story with readers everywhere! If you have an adventure in public speaking that you'd like to share, send it to: treyguinn.com/adventuresinpublicspeaking.

Story 1: Introductions are really important.

Not all that long ago, I got a call from a friend of mine that is a leader at a telecommunications company. Her budget was spent, but major changes were hitting her organization, and she wanted to know if I would do her a favor and come facilitate a morale boosting workshop for her team of about 20.

It was going to be a three-hour workshop just before Thanksgiving. Under normal circumstances, I would have charged top dollar to develop and deliver a three-hour workshop for a major telecommunications company, especially around the holidays when I try to reserve that time for family. But the date that she needed me worked with my schedule, and I was happy to help a friend. So, I said yes.

I was rushed that day, and I arrived on-site with only 30 minutes to spare. I met my friend outside the conference site of the event. The participants were inside eating lunch before our session. She walked me in to survey the room. I couldn't see a projector and screen, so I asked how the technology was going to work. She told me, "Oh, you wouldn't believe what they were going to charge me for that, so I hope you are ok to go without tech."

As you can imagine, giving a pro bono talk for three hours without the benefit of using the slides I prepared for the event was less than desirable. But that was ok. I don't mind a challenge. I walked outside and strategized a new game plan really quick.

I came back in, poured a coffee (fortunately, their budget could afford all the coffee that I was going to need!), and sat down with the group as they wrapped up their lunch. My friend had told me that she would do an introduction, and that would be my cue to get started.

Her speech to introduce me to the audience, which I gather was meant to be funny, went something like this:

Hey, hope you liked lunch. Denise picked it. So, if you didn't like it, blame her, not me. (No one laughed.)

On a serious note, though, we're having major changes at work. We all feel them, and it's not all that fun. So, I wanted today to be a time where we could come together, discuss all the changes, and develop some new protocols for how to manage them. We accomplished this during the morning session. Then, I wanted us to have some lunch together. And later, I really wanted us to have some meaningful time this afternoon to really bond as a team, maybe even be inspired. So, I tried to get us one of those fancy, expensive speakers... but, we all know that we have no budget, so... this is what we got – Trey. (She pointed to me.)

(Again, no one laughed) Some of you already know Trey from other work he has done with us. And yeah, Trey, the floor is yours.

Honest to goodness, while I may have missed the precise language, that was the gist of her introduction of me. I don't think she meant any harm. I truly believe she was trying to be funny, but it flopped, and it left people in the room confused. I could see their faces as I was seated amongst them. They didn't know what to think. Unless they had magically guessed that she was being humorous, for all they knew, the next three-hours with me were going to be awful, and not even the person in charge of the event wanted me there.

The seating was a U-shape, and I made my way to the top of the U. I said how glad I was to be there with them all, especially as they made sense of some turbulent times. I then made a joke saying, "What my friend doesn't know is that her boss promised me and my family a lifetime of free internet, cable, and phones, which is far better than a one-time speaker's fee." The crowd ate it up. I then talked a little bit about how I enjoy working with companies during change management and that, while there are similar experiences, no two stories are the same. Within two minutes, I had undone the horrible introduction and setup that I was given.

Experiences like this one urge me to remind you of two things:

First, when giving a speech of introduction, always set the presenter up for success.

Ask if they have something prepared that they want you to use when introducing them. If not, ask them for some general direction about how they want to be introduced. Your job is to alley-oop the presenter—toss the ball up in the perfect spot so that all they have to do is grab the ball and slam dunk.

If you do your introduction well, the audience will be confident in the credibility of the speaker, and then it is up to the speaker to maintain, possibly elevate, the credibility you provided them.

Second, when presenting somewhere, be thoughtful about the speech of introduction you want given on your behalf, and don't be afraid to ask, perhaps even insist, that it be used.

Your speech of introduction should not overpromise what you will deliver during the talk. Instead, it should highlight why you are the perfect person to present to this crowd about the given subject that day. The presenter should not have to sell that point. It is far better and more believable when done for you.

A great speech of introduction should leave little to no doubt in the minds of your audience that you are the right person to give the presentation that you are about to deliver.

Story 2: Be not dismayed by Netflix face.

For the past few years, I have noticed an alarming trend. Audiences look more bored and act more bored than they used to. It's the wildest thing. I started noticing it around 2015 or so, but people's facial affect and laughs are more muted than they used to be. And it is not just me. My clients are commenting that they feel as though they are presenting to dead audiences, but then they will receive positive feedback after a talk. It's been a mystery to me.

But I think I finally solved the mystery. I call it Netflix face. Whether I am on a plane, sitting in a doctor's office waiting room, or even eating somewhere, I notice more and more that people sit alone and watch their media of choice on their smartphone with earbuds. It doesn't matter what they are watching, their faces all look the same; they look like somebody in their robe standing at the coffee maker—half awake, unamused. They could be watching a comedian, but you rarely hear a laugh. They could be watching a horror film, yet you never see them jump or wince. A sad movie, but you never see them cry.

Our society has developed a new skill for having muted responses to media. Perhaps it is because laughing alone seems awkward. Certainly, when others around us are laughing, we feel freer to laugh louder. But I think muted responses might be due also to our desire to not draw attention or disturb the room. We consume media individually while in communal spaces, so now it seems impolite to laugh out loud when something is funny or begin crying in public. We are daily training ourselves to consume media and entertainment in isolation, where generations before us did so in community— as a family in the living room, at the theatre with a hundred others, and so on.

Pre-smartphones and before the days of Netflix, if I delivered an entertaining, interactive, and engaging presentation, I could expect that my audience would respond with communal smiles, laughter, applause, and more. Now, the default response of my audience is Netflix face.

After a presentation, however, scores of people walk up and say things like, "Wow, great job. Loved your talk." And the emails pour in, "You were awesome. We'd love to have you come speak to…."

This, of course, seems bazar given that these individuals appeared half-asleep during the duration of the presentation. Could they be lying? I've come to believe not. I believe they do love it; they just don't remember how to show it. They see someone take the stage and they settle into Netflix face, as if they were binge watching on a plane.

I share this not to judge or shame society, but to warn presenters so that they not be too frightened by Netflix face.

When you get five minutes into your presentation and see people autopilot into Netflix face, they may, in fact, be thrilled to hear you speak. When you walk around the room and people don't perk up with big smiles, they may be fully engaged but forget how to show it. You must remain calm, confident, and present your best.

One of my best friends writes music and performs regularly. Any given gig, he might be performing to thousands of people at a time. On occasion, however, I have been with him when he is performing to much smaller venues. I remember days when he'd play at a coffeeshop of 20 people sipping lattes and only partly listening to him and his band. One time, I asked him what it was like to switch from one venue to another and how he gets himself to play his heart out when people are hardly listening. He admitted that it was hard and that there are occasions where a member of the band will start to go low energy because of small crowd size or lack of audience involvement. But he reminded me that you can't do that. He likened it to a boomerang—you never get back what you don't first throw out there.

The moment you go low energy or lack in enthusiasm, it's over. The audience will never give you high energy, enthusiasm, and involvement if you aren't committed to giving it to them first. So, no matter what your audience is doing, you must present 110%.

Most often, they like you and what you are doing but just don't know how to show it. You've got to stick with it, at least until you can find one or two people in the room that will give you their eye contact and nod their heads. Let that positive feedback loop fill your soul, and then build off of it. Before long, you will have a patch of people that are sticking with you and staying engaged. Keep them involved and reward their involvement with big smiles and lots of eye contact so that others will wish for it too. And then overtake the room!

Story 3: Know your role; play your part

A couple years back, a mid-sized tech firm found me through a referral. They scheduled a call to see if I would be willing to travel to this river resort to give the farewell talk and group workshop on the final morning of a weekend business retreat. The talk they wanted was right up my alley, and they sounded like a neat group, so I was happy to do it.

Communication leading up to the event was great. The point of contact was on the ball. She was even sending me travel details well in advance—pictures of the room that I'd be speaking in, names and functional roles of all the participants. This group seemed great and very organized! I began imagining that this group might be suit, tie, and all business. So, I made sure to bring a lot of resources and tokens that would symbolize my business side, just in case they needed it.

The morning of the event, I make my way to the room where I will be speaking. The point of contact was there to greet me and get me situated. She seemed friendly but a little slower moving than I expected. Her boss, the president of the company, arrived to meet me as well. He was teasing her about something from the day before, and I noticed that he was sunburned. More people showed up with breakfast in hand. One guy asked if anyone had Advil. Everyone was wearing casual clothes, from board shorts to jeans.

People were giggling, and some were groggy. It finally dawned on me: most of these people were hungover, and this whole weekend was a big corporate party. They didn't want a content-heavy keynote. They wanted me to sing a farewell song.

So, I spoke to my point of contact very calmly and said, "Looks like everyone has had a good time this weekend, and I'd love to help keep spirits high. Given what we know right now, would you advise that I focus on fun stuff, like making people laugh and just making sure that everyone has a good time?" She shook her head yes enthusiastically. And so, I did. I threw out the prepared presentation and played the court jester for 90 minutes. Everyone had a blast, including me.

The reason the situation worked is two-fold:

One, before a presentation, I never read my notes; instead, I read my audience.

Remember, these people determine whether you reach your goal.

Two, I remain nimble, and allow the goal and my role to change as needed.

Once I read my crowd, I realized all preconceived notions and discussions about this event were to be thrown out the window. I needed to wise-up and re-examine the situation. Doing so helped me to better know my role and play my part.

Story 4: Feedback can hurt. Listen anyway and learn what you need to learn.

Some years back, I was invited to speak to first-year MBA students at a top 10 business school in the country. This is a pretty regular type of talk and crowd for me. And I'd always had great experiences speaking on this campus before. I was pretty excited about the talk.

About 30-minutes before start time, I received a call requesting for major changes to the content and slide deck. Apparently, the organizers were not in agreement on the learning outcomes for the talk. Not an ideal situation, but I was happy to oblige.

Minutes before the talk, I asked my assistant to walk around the auditorium and come back with a read on the room. She returns to say, "Well, the people I'm listening in on don't seem thrilled to be here." I asked why. And she continued, "They all seem pretty bummed because apparently this is a required event for them happening during the middle of their midterms. And some other people were talking about how they had to cancel important meetings to be on campus for this talk."

Ok, so I figured that I had my work cut out for me. A stadium full of people that have been forced to attend and would rather be somewhere else. Not ideal, but I can adjust. I think to myself that I should go 110% on energy and then delight them by ending a few minutes earlier than planned.

With only a minute or two from go-time, I learned that the guy who was supposed to walk out and do my introduction had gone missing. The lady coordinating the event had insisted that I get started and just do my own introduction, which is fine; I certainly didn't need an introduction. When doing my own, I avoid talking about myself and simply emphasize what a privilege it is to be there. The downside for that, with this particular audience, was that they didn't want to be there, so a few words from someone else about how wonderful I am could have potentially helped make the case for why they should want to be there and pay attention.

I got started to no welcome applause, and it became obvious to me in the first few minutes of presenting that this group of 250+ was more committed to emails and spreadsheets on their laptops than listening to a presentation on how to become a best-in-class presenter. So, I called an audible and started playing interactive scenarios and games with volunteers from the audience. I figured the room would enjoy seeing their peers with me on stage, and it did boost attention. Within minutes, the room was engaged.

At the two-hour mark, I decided to end the presentation a little early and go straight into question and answer time. I got some good questions and fielded them well. The audience gave moderate applause and I felt "good enough" about the presentation given the circumstances—major changes to content by the organizer within an hour of start time, zero introduction for my talk, and a room of people who didn't want to be there.

Immediately following the event, I had good feedback from people that wanted my contact information and hoped to do some follow-up work with me. That was nice. I also had one person that walked up to share they disagreed with something I said. I listened, but the line was growing, so I offered to buy us lunch next time I was in town so that we could finish the conversation. Instead, we ended up having a phone call later in the week, and I learned a really valuable perspective. So, I was grateful for that.

Then, about a week later, the organizer for the event called me to talk about the presentation. I falsely expected that I would hear, "Thanks for all you did and being so adaptable with all those curveballs." I had worked with these people for nearly a decade and heard zero praise for the event. It was kind of a, "You know we love working with you, but..." and then came a bombshell. They continued, "We've had some complaints about something you said. Do you remember a man that came on stage with you—De'Mon?"

Of course I did. He was hilarious, and our impromptu bit together was the funniest part of the day! In fact, we stayed in contact and ended up working together.

They continued, "Well, some people were very bothered when

you said, 'You da man, De'Mon!'" I asked for an explanation of why and the response tore my heart.

I was floored. My jaw dropped. For context of when the statement was said, he and I had just finished an impromptu game on the stage that was absolutely hysterical. The whole room was laughing. I asked the crowd to give it up for De'Mon. They did. Clapping and cheering for him ensued. As he was walking back to his seat, he looks back and shouted something funny at me, and I pointed back saying, "It was all you. You da man, De'Mon!" And then we carried on with the next part of the presentation. After the show, De'Mon came up and talked with me for a quick minute. He was a super nice guy and even thanked me for a great talk.

Now, a week after the event, the feedback from the organizers of the event is not that I saved the day on an event that was crumbling, it's that there were complaints from people in the audience about the "you da man" exchange with De'Mon. Some people in the audience felt that it demonstrated racial insensitivity. I was asked the question, "Well, would you have said that to a white guy?" The answer is yes! And I have thousands of times—it's a generational phrase, something I grew up hearing and saying everywhere, that crossed skin tones. And in this case, the guy's name was the perfect play on words for me to say it.

But defending myself would have been a waste. At the end of the day, this wasn't about my heart and my intent; it was about the impact. The damage had been done. The message I intended to send was not the one that some people received.

I'll avoid elaborating on how much this feedback hurt me at the core. It did. God and my wife know just how much that feedback hurt my heart. In fact, sharing this story now feels very vulnerable and kind of hurts. But, ultimately, that's why I share the story.

After I received that feedback, I remember telling my wife that I never wanted to give another presentation. It hurt so bad that I never wanted to experience something like that again. She talked sense into me, reminded me to take some of my own advice:

Learn what you need to learn, and keep moving.

So, for the day—if it ever happens—that you receive really painful feedback, remember that is what may come from taking the stage, being in the arena. You will be evaluated not just on your intent, but also on your impact; how your words and behaviors impact a person's thoughts, feelings, and behaviors.

Was I intending to trigger anyone negatively? Absolutely not. But was someone(s) in the room bothered by what I said?

Yes. And that is enough for me to listen, learn what I need to learn, and grow as I need to grow from the situation.

I hope that you will do the same. I hope that you will learn to filter feedback well. Hear what you need to hear so that you can learn what you need to learn. Then, filter out those particles that sting and hurt without just cause.

I remember when I was younger and just getting started as a presenter. I'd hear ore read little pieces of feedback like, "He seems too young," or, "What does he know? He's half our age and has never done our job." I couldn't control my age (so I had to let go of that), but I could dress a little older, and I could build in some purposeful refutation strategies. I learned to adapt and incorporate feedback in meaningful ways, while also filtering out the stuff that I couldn't control.

Similarly, from the "you da man" experience, I learned to be mindful of the fact that:

My audience can't see my heart, but they can hear my words and see my actions. How can I ensure that my heart translates through my words and actions?

Enhancing your presentational effectiveness will require filtering feedback well. Here is wishing you and me great success in that effort!

Story 5: Always fail forward.

Very early in my career as a presenter, I was invited to speak to one of the major consulting firms. They hired me to give two talks. A morning talk to senior leadership that would focus on executive presence and crisis communication, and an afternoon talk to data analysts and junior associates.

Admittedly, I was pretty excited about these two talks. As described to me, the senior leadership talk was to be a highly interactive engagement with just a handful of selected leaders; a chance to do some in-depth work on some specific skill areas. The second talk was also designed to be a highly interactive engagement, but to a large group of mostly entry-level and recent MBA graduates that would appreciate some confidence-boosting and presentational-polishing for when speaking to senior leaders and clients.

My excitement grew as the day was drawing nearer. I even called one of my best buddies on the way to the site and told him that I felt like I was living a dream.

Except my dream soon turned to a nightmare. I walked into the bottom floor of the skyscraper and called my point of contact to alert her that I had arrived. She met me at the coffee shop and asked if we could get a coffee before heading up.

Over coffee, she proceeded to tell me how thrilled they were that I was onsite to speak to the groups but that the senior leadership talk was postponed due to poor planning on her part; this particular Friday turned out to be a day when all the senior leaders were out of office, either still at client sites or otherwise working remotely. I would still get payed for that talk, but it would just be postponed for a later date. Ok, no big deal, I thought.

We took the long elevator ride to the top floor. She showed me around office suites that looked fit for a queen. Someone rushed in to whisk her away, and so she left me in a waiting area for what felt like eternity. No problem, as the views were incredible.

When she returned, she ushered me to a different part of the building, informing me that the talk to the large group would now be held in a private conference room. When we arrived, I discovered it was an elegant room with great views and a long wooden table that took up the whole room—at most, you could squeeze 20 people inside.

Just as we enter the room, she takes a call and promises me she will return quickly. The presentation was scheduled to start in five minutes, and I didn't see anyone in sight or even know where to plug in my laptop.

It was now 1-minute past the start time, and I was the only person in the room. No sign of life and no clue as to how I am to set-up. I was standing around clueless. Eventually, two people entered the room wearing earpieces and holding their laptops open. They were finishing client calls and responding to emails. I tried to make small talk as they ended their calls, but they were preoccupied.

Five minutes into the presentation start time, I finally peeked out the room to find my point of contact and politely asked for some clarification about what was happening. Apparently, the session was being recorded and had been since I arrived. Huh? Say what? Aside from the conference phone in the middle of the table, I saw zero signs of technology. I asked if we were waiting on more people. She suggested that with time already running out, I should just get started.

I have been thrown some curveballs before, but I was legitimately lost this time. I felt like I had taken crazy pills. Was I supposed to start presenting? To whom, and how? Fortunately, she came inside the room, and so I just winged it and started presenting to her, encouraging the other two in the room on their laptops to join us for the presentation.

I tried to go with the plans that I had prepared. I got five minutes in (and it was going ok), but then I just felt everything falling apart. I still couldn't figure out where the camera was, but I knew the event was being recorded. I had prepared an interactive session for 100+ people, but there were only three people in the room, all of them multitasking on their laptops. **Apparently, I had not yet mastered the art of being nimble.**

I went another five minutes of presenting to a lifeless room, and I could feel myself sweating profusely. I paused myself mid-sentence and asked my point of contact for a moment to chat in the hallway. We stepped outside and I said, "Look, thanks for having me, but this is clearly not the presentation we had planned for. The audience of you plus two clearly have other things to be doing. I can't waste any more time—yours or mine. No hard feelings on my part. You all can keep the speaker's fee, and let's just call it a day."

She said that she respected my decision but asked if I would give her a minute to talk with the group. I honestly didn't want to see any of them again; I just wanted to get home. So, I took a long, slow walk up and down the hallway before returning to the conference room, where to my surprise there were now 15 people filling the conference table. Where were all these people half an hour ago? I figured they arrived for another meeting, so I went to collect my bag and wish them a good weekend.

The group was smiling at me very politely and offered their apologies for being absent and otherwise disengaged. They said I was free to leave if I chose but that they hoped I would stay a little longer and answer some of their questions. I felt like I was in the Twilight Zone.

I took a seat at the head of the conference table, learned each of their names, and invited their questions for what became a fruitful 90-minute discussion with 15 bright business leaders. They asked me important questions about things like leading-up to their supervisors, managing conflict with colleagues, and how to persuade clients toward unpopular opinions. It was not at all the presentation I prepared, but it became something meaningful anyway.

While the situation was ultimately redeemed, to be clear: I initially failed at being nimble and adapting to the situation. I got freaked, crumbled under the circumstances, and pulled the plug on a presentation.

Did they set me up for failure? *Yes.*

Should that matter? *Nope.*

As the presenter, it's always on me to be nimble, rise to the occasion, and get the job done.

Knowing what I know now, I should have read the room and adapted by doing as they ultimately invited me to do in the end—pulling up a seat and starting a conversation with the individuals that were present. I could have sold it as a special small group discussion with some in-depth activities intended for high potential leaders. It would have been awesome had I done that!

But I didn't. Instead, I violated my own rules for presentational effectiveness. I got caught up in all the oddities of the moment and forgot to be nimble.

Fortunately for me that day, the lady in charge snapped, got more people in the room, and I had a chance to come back and redeem myself. And I am grateful she did because in the midst of my feelings of failure, shock, and humility, I was forced to get back in the arena and go again.

After being totally knocked down, I was given an opportunity to adapt, try again, and find a path to victory. And in doing so, I discovered new levels of resilience as a presenter.

The totality of events that day felt extremely bazar at the time, but they instilled in me a realization that if I remain calm and confident and operate nimbly, I can manage any speaking situation thrown my way. Though I failed, I managed to fail forward. The moment was redeemed, and I left the building that day humbled and strengthened for the better. I look back at that event as one of the critical learnings in my life as a presenter.

I learned that no matter what, I can and will **be nimble, rise to the occasion, and get the job done!**

NOTES

While the thoughts presented here have been inspired by many individuals and their brilliant work, I explicitly referenced only a handful of scholars inside this book. If you wish to learn more about any of them, I encourage you to follow the links here:

- Dr. John Daly, along with Dr. James McCroskey, were two of the scholars that pioneered the study of communication apprehension (e.g., willingness to communicate). You can learn about Dr. Daly and his scholarship by going here: https://commstudies.utexas.edu/faculty/john-daly

- Dr. Carol Dweck is the author of Mindset. You can learn more about her and her scholarship by going here: https://profiles.stanford.edu/carol-dweck

- Barbara Minto developed the Pyramid Principle that helps people discover and clarify the points they wish to make. You can learn more about her and her work by going here: http://www.barbaraminto.com/

SELECTED WORKS

Adventures in Adulting
        Trey Guinn (Author)
        Shannon Guinn (Illustrator)

*Be: Embracing childlike wonder and the truth of who
we are through short stories*
        Shannon Guinn (Author, Illustrator)
        William Marshall (Editor)
        Trey Guinn (Contributor)

Doggy Discovers Gratitude
        Shannon Guinn (Author, Illustrator)
        Trey Guinn (Author)

Enhancing Presentational Effectiveness
        Trey Guinn (Author)
        Shannon Guinn (Illustrator)

ABOUT THE AUTHOR

Dr. Trey Guinn and his family reside in Texas. A university professor and department chair, Guinn is also an active author, actor, speaker, executive coach and consultant to clients globally. A key focus of his work is on human development, communication effectiveness, and personal relationships. Friends say the secret to his positivity and success is an attitude of gratitude, abiding faith, love for others, in addition to lots of running and coffee!

treyguinn.com

Made in the USA
Coppell, TX
05 December 2020